Train Your Mind to Be Successful

*Attract and Get Everything
You Want in Life*

Sayra S. Montes

Train Your Mind to Be Successful. Attract and get anything you want in life.

Published by Sayra S. Montes
Mexicali, Baja California, Mexico

Copyright ©2020 Sayra S. Montes. All rights reserved.

No part of this book may be reproduced in any form or by any mechanical means, including information storage and retrieval systems without permission in writing from the publisher/author, except by a reviewer who may quote passages in a review.

All images, logos, quotes, and trademarks included in this book are subject to use according to trademark and copyright laws of United States.

MONTES, SAYRA S., Author
TRAIN YOUR MIND TO BE SUCCESSFUL
SAYRA S. MONTES

ISBN: 978-0-578-91222-6

QUANTITY PURCHASES: Schools, companies, professional groups, clubs, and other organizations may qualify for special terms when ordering quantities of this title.

For information, email sayramontes02@hotmail.com.

All rights reserved by SAYRA S. MONTES.

This book is printed in United States.

To my dearest students.
Thank you for making me better each day.

CONTENTS

Introduction..

Chapter 1: The Early Birds' Club..

Chapter 2: Positive Mind, Positive Results.................................1

Chapter 3: Dream Big..2

Chapter 4: Visualize It...2

Chapter 5: Attract It...4

Chapter 6: The Power of Belief...4

Chapter 7: Change Your Mindset..5

Chapter 8: Be good to yourself..7

Chapter 9: Environment...8

Chapter 10: Goal Setting..8

Chapter 11: Go Hard or Go Home...9

Chapter 12: Take a Break..9

Chapter 13: Be Teachable..10

Chapter 14: Abundance and Prosperity.....................................10

Chapter 15: The Power of Silence...11

Chapter 16: Take Action..12

Chapter 17: Write It Up...13

v

Introduction

Training your mind and achieving success is something we never seem to learn in school. Through neuroplasticity, we can learn new things and channel our brain to think and act in a particular way, but that is only the beginning. With new connections comes learning, which becomes a part of our thought processes, which is formulated with the mind. The mind plays a major role in achieving major, minor, daily, and long-term goals while setting you on the path of success.

It is easier for most human beings to achieve minor goals that come day to day because the mind can only go that far. When it comes to major goals, it is a whole new ball game, and only a truly trained mind can thrive.

To satisfy the intense hunger and thirst for accomplishment and success, requires the skillful use of your mind power. To focus and truly excel, you need to be able to set your eyes on the prize. The key to accomplishing those clear ideas is in the mind. Every word making up this book will be a key to unlocking the mind-power role in achieving success in life. The truth is that success is 20% skills and 80% psychology.

Think of the brain as an organ—a tool to achieve your goals. The brain is the hardware, while the mind is the software. To achieve your goals, the software must be up and running, and we know that the software is the most delicate and important part in any sophisticated computer. We are well aware that a crash in the hardware should be easily salvaged, but a tiny hitch in the software system could lead to the complete downfall of the entire system. That is how the mind works in propelling you to achieve those goals you crave so badly.

Everything is observed and developed in the mind; it is where the magic happens, but a lot of people pay little attention to it. The mind is like a double-edged sword, if used properly. It is your ultimate tool to success, but a single mistake can send you running down the hill. Studies show we think up to 80,000 thoughts a day. These thoughts can work constructively to push you to achieve your goals or tear you down in the worst possible way, even if you have the best of intentions. If you constantly tear yourself down, it will begin to manifest in your life. The things we think and the thoughts we welcome into our minds are the biggest agents that can make or break us.

"Whatever you sow, you will reap." That pretty much explains it. People often say that whatever you think is what you become. It is only logical. If you sow thoughts that will move you to the point of success, you reap success in return, and vice versa. Thoughts influence actions, and actions eventually determine how you turn out in life, so it all stems from your thoughts, which is processed in the mind; hence, there is the need to train your mind. Yes, you can change your life and achieve your goals, but it begins with training your mind to achieve that success.

The human mind is what makes us different from other creatures. The brain—the hardware—is visibly present in other animals. Our complex and unfathomable mind is what sets us apart and places us on a pedestal. Training and sharpening it is the heavy burden that rests on our shoulders as human beings. Everything we are, all up till today, all started with a thought/idea in the mind. The mind is where calculation, reasoning, and decision-making take place. We are constantly making decisions—no matter how little—and these decisions, taken in the mind, have slowly worked together to build the person we are today.

Success, in fact, is relative. What constitutes victory in life for one person completely differs from the next, but that is okay. Everybody lives in their own personal worlds, each placing value on different aspects of life. Some people see money as the greatest metric for success, while others pursue happiness. The side that people lean towards is dependent on many factors, including living standards and past trauma, yet one thing remains the same: everyone strives towards something.

Train Your Mind to Be Successful teaches readers how to change their mindsets to better their chances of reaching their dreams. Everyone's goals differ, but with the right mentality, anybody can achieve their ideal life. Whether you strive for improvement at work, in your finances, or your relationships, the best place to start is within yourself.

Personal betterment is something that almost everyone wishes to accomplish, but few people ever actually try. Knowing where to start is often the most intimidating part of the journey, and the mere thought of wetting their feet is enough to scare most people away. A small amount of the population ever reaches their goals, and that is not a mistake. Most people simply lack the motivation required to get anywhere in life, something that can be attributed to a widespread mindset that is wired for failure.

Some people work 15 hours per day and still barely make ends meet. Some people have millions of dollars, but they are not happy and fulfilled. Some people live at the gym and still are not satisfied with their bodies.

When it comes to finding success, the journey is often more beneficial than the destination. While there is nothing quite like crushing your goals, there is something to be said about the climb. Learning to love the road to success and developing a hunger for the journey will not only make the whole process more enjoyable, but it will also dampen the discouragement when failure rears its head. This book provides expert insight into altering your mentality for success.

Chasing dreams can sometimes seem impossible. Regardless of their magnitude, the goals we set for ourselves mockingly glare at us, increasing the pressure to succeed and the embarrassment that surrounds failure. If your goals seem unattainable, this book is for you. The truth of the matter is that success is not guaranteed, and often it is not likely, but switching your approach can greatly increase your odds of reaching your goals. *Train Your Mind to Be Successful* is your blueprint to do so.

CHAPTER 1

The Early Birds' Club

"When you arise in the morning, think of what a precious privilege it is to be alive - to breathe, to think, to enjoy, to love."

— **Marcus Aurelius**

You wake up every day, prepare and set out for the day's activities, and deal with the different tasks of the day, but before the day runs out, you are already feeling beat up, stressed and overwhelmed. Before the end of the week, you are already feeling fatigued and unable to meet your target for the week. This is the situation most people find themselves in, but there is a way out through what is referred to as a productive routine.

Research has shown that most people perform the best in the early hours of the day after waking up from sleep. This is linked to the fact that the brain and body have been rested and refreshed from peaceful and quality sleep. When you first wake, you are in the alpha state, which means that your brain operates at around 10.5 waves per second.

Successful people do not immediately check e-mails after waking up. They claim the first hours of the day as "their" time, devoting themselves to what is very important in their own scale of values.

Three years ago, I started getting curious about what successful people were doing to make themselves succeed. Reading books, watching videos, and listening to other people talking about how having a morning routine helped them get all their daily activities done led me to put that information to practice. I used to be a non-morning person. I remember when I was in college, arriving late to all my classes, not giving a damn about being on time anywhere I went, not respecting other people's time and always thinking about how horrible and detestable it was waking up so early. "How does waking up this early in the morning benefit me?" I thought. The result was a little surprising for me. When I started taking care of my physique, I did not have enough time to work out in the evening, so I decided to go to the gym in the morning at 5 am before going to work, because I really wanted to be healthy and in shape. I realized how well my days became and how productive they were. I was feeling so active and focused. Research shows that working out in the morning enhances your metabolism, helps you to cultivate consistency, leads you to be more disciplined and improves your mental and physical energy. Now, I wake up every day at 5 am. I go to work, I do not arrive late anymore, and I follow a routine that has been helping me since then, without a doubt, to get better every day. Actually, my students ask me almost every day how I look so happy and motivated when it's only 7 a.m. You need to ask yourself: What is a routine I can adopt and follow to become more effective, proactive, and productive?

Wake up early: Time is an invaluable advantage. The most effective and productive people do not hesitate to get up at 5:30 am, 4:30 am or even 4 am. As you wake up early, not only will you have more control over your early hours, but you will also have more opportunities to do the things that really matter to you. Start waking up 15 minutes ahead of your usual time until you reach the wake-up time you have set for yourself. If that looks difficult for you, you can try to jump out of bed immediately after counting backwards from 5 to 1. This approach works very well in the military, but if you want a long-term change and make it a habit, try to get out of bed 5 minutes after opening your eyes. You will be calm and more focused. Waking up early to invest these early hours of the day into self-development can set the tone and greatly impact your productivity for the day. Waking up early gives you sufficient time to go through your morning routine without pressure or the rush to meet up to time. A new day requires a new, healthy start.

Be thankful: Remember to adore every single thing you possess; embrace every situation, either is good or bad; appreciate the people who have been with you through ups and downs. After waking up, list or think about all the things you are thankful for. You will create an opportunity to remind yourself how fortunate you are. By doing this, you will avoid taking for granted the privileges you enjoy, you will be more open to optimism and you will get a positive vision of life. Write at least three things for which you are grateful for every day. Learn to keep memories of every little success. If you don't have enough time to write because you are in a hurry on your way to work or school, take a few seconds and say thank you for three things you are thankful for at that moment; it could be anything. Feel free to change your list every day. For example: I am thankful for my job; it allows me to learn something new every day and to earn money. I am thankful for having another day of life; this is a new day with new opportunities to grow. I am thankful for my family; they always support me no matter what happens...and so on. You can think it or write it down on a notebook. Instead of starting your day complaining how much you hate waking up early, going to work, the traffic, and dealing with your annoying co-workers, switch your negative thoughts into positive ones and realize how favored you are.

Make your bed: A simple habit, like making your bed in the morning, can make a difference. In 2014, in a commencement speech at the University of Austin, Texas, the commander of U.S. Special Operations., Naval Admiral William McRaven, shared his thoughts. "If you make your bed every morning, you will have accomplished the first task of the day. It will give you a small sense of pride, and it will encourage you to do another task and another and another," he said. "Making your bed will also reinforce the fact that little things in life matter." Making up your bed also can improve your productivity. Author Charles Duhigg, in his book, *The Power of Habit*, expresses that daily bed-making becomes a keystone habit, something that kickstarts a chain of other good decisions throughout the day, giving you a sense of taking charge. Making it a habit will develop more good habits. Having a clean environment is important; it shows you have a clearer vision of everything. And last but not least, you want to start your day with success. How you do anything is how you do everything.

Drink water: Your brain is 80% water. You lose a lot of water when you are sleeping, and many people are dehydrated. It is important for your brain to stay hydrated to function at its best. Grab a cup of water before starting your day. It will jump-start your metabolism, eliminate toxins, improve skin health, improve mental performance, and reduce your calorie intake throughout the day as it increases your feelings of fullness.

Ask yourself an important question: "If today was the last day of my life, would I still doing what I'm about to do today?" This not an easy question, but this definitely helps you to understand where you are in your life and where you want to be. If you find yourself saying "no" several times in a week, then it is time to get busy and start changing something. You never know when you will have the chance to do it next time.

Journaling: If you don't take a few minutes of your time to chart the direction of the day, how will you know if you are on the right path? Take at least 10 minutes in the morning to check your goals of the day and to organize your free time. This will help you manage your day more effectively and less stressfully. Use this journal to list what you are grateful for as well. Leonardo DaVinci, Albert Einstein, Marie Curie and many others had a journal and practiced journaling every day to increase their imagination and to have a path to follow.

Burn calories: I don't just mean an intense training regimen with this: you can simply do yoga or stretch. Go for a run, a walk or whatever you feel like doing. Exercise will not only help you maintain a state of physical and mental well-being, but it will also allow you to fight stress. Try taking some time in the morning to devote to physical activity. If a one-hour routine seems too daunting, then start with 15-20 minutes and gradually increase. If you don't have time for a whole routine, take 3 to 4 minutes to increase your blood pressure and get more oxygen in your brain. You can choose between jumping jacks, crunches, squats, or whatever is on your option list.

Tidy up the clutter: In the morning, willpower is at its highest level and is ready to give the best of itself. This is the best time to take advantage of it and to dedicate yourself to your most difficult task, the project or the thing that grips your mind the most. In this way, with fresh energy, without any distractions and interruptions from other people, it will be easier to carry it out. As much as you can, do not leave the clutters of the day into the next day; it will be a bad way to start off your tomorrow. Ditch the procrastination and spend a few minutes tidying up and clearing out the clutter. This will leave you feeling happy and accomplished.

Avoid social media: Social media has its pros and cons. Unfortunately, research has shown that social media causes anxiety, depression, loneliness, and it drives you to distraction and procrastination. If you have a social media addiction, you should try to stay away from it at least in the morning or the first hour after waking up. If you start your day checking your Instagram, Facebook or Twitter, you will find bad news, you will be wondering why your crush hasn't texted you yet or why you haven't reached a certain number of likes on Facebook or Instagram. On the other hand, we know social media is used mostly to feed people's egos and is something that produces dopamine. If you feed your ego with social media first thing in the morning, there's a chance it will continue to require feeding throughout the day. If you start off your day with social media, there is a huge chance you will spend more time on it. Instead, choose to grab a book and dedicate your morning time to feeding your brain.

Meditate. Give yourself a few minutes each morning to reconnect with the most intimate and profound part of yourself. Meditate, pray, repeat a mantra, follow your breath, or do what you prefer as long as it helps you to connect with your deepest self. Remember that 90% of illnesses are related to stress, so forget about hurry, don't rush yourself and enjoy a few moments of "silence" with yourself. You can start meditating 5 minutes a day. Meditating has positive effects on our bodies and our health. It also helps to have a clearer vision of everything around us, about what we really want and how we feel at the moment. You can choose this time to visualize your dreams as well.

CHAPTER 2

Positive Mind, Positive Results

"I always knew I was a writer. And I always thought to myself, 'Well, why not me?' Someone has to be on the bestseller list, 'Why not me?' Someone has to write for the 'New Yorker,' 'Why not me?' And I didn't really get much positive reinforcement as a kid, so I thought, 'Well let me show you what I can do."

— **Elizabeth Wurtzel**

You have probably heard the word "positive mindset" mentioned, perhaps during motivational talk sessions or during other success-focused presentations, and it may sometimes feel like it is a cliché. You may have even heard of how it is an effective key to success without knowing exactly what it means. So, what does it really mean to have a positive mindset? A positive mindset, just like other skills, may not come naturally, but it can be learned. There are people who naturally have a positive and happy disposition. Other people, however, must develop conscious efforts to learn and practice having positive mental attitude. Developing a positive mindset will require an individual to accept positive thoughts, positive images, positive words, and positive feelings into their mind and ponder on them as well. It means that you will constantly scrutinize what kind of energy you allow around you, as this can influence how you react to situations that may arise.

There are many famous entrepreneurs who claim to have arrived where they are, thanks to the adoption of positive thinking within their lifestyle. A person who relates to life with a positive approach will always have greater success—both in his professional life and in his personal life—than one who has no control over his thoughts. This is a fact, not a new age belief.

The topic has attracted the attention of major business magazines, and a number of authoritative scientific studies have been conducted to support the benefits of positive thinking. But what is positive thinking? How can we adapt it to our professional life? How can we benefit from it?

In the professional field, we find that *productivity* and *success* are the most-used words with positive connotations. Positive thinking helps you at work, school or in your life in general. How are happiness and productivity connected? How can practicing positive thoughts improve your productivity? It is not necessary to look beyond your mental approach. People who enjoy what they do are way more productive than those who are not passionate about their jobs.

Have you ever been doing something for hours that you really enjoy, and it felt like a few minutes? That happens when you really like what you do.

Psychological tests show that happy people have some special quality that enables them to have a better life. Happy people tend to be successful because of their way of thinking. They find the good in the bad for every situation. They laugh at their problems like they are nothing and make jokes about it. They do not complain, because they know there is always a solution. They are willing to go through awkward, sad and embarrassing situations, and they enjoy and trust the process of growing and becoming the better version of themselves.

We have seen many people around us, living such a pitiful life due to their negative thoughts and behaviors. Just think about that co-worker who is always hating on everyone for no reason, that one who spends energy and time gossiping and giving a non-requested opinion about other people's life. There might be something wrong with them. The more energy you waste on negative stuff, the more negative stuff you'll get. The more positive energy you spend, the happier life you'll live.

Do you want to be happy? Start acting happy: say what happy people say, do and behave like them, change your perspective, practice positive thoughts and you will get amazing results.

It might seem difficult changing your mentality from negative to positive, but as a positive individual, I guarantee you this exercise is life changing. In developing a positive mindset, there are different ways an individual can explore to develop a positive mindset, but the first step is to dump negative thoughts. Make a conscious effort to eliminate negative thoughts from your mind. If you fail to drop negative thoughts from your mind, you will be unable to build a positive mindset and will never see the positives within negative situations.

Experts have found that to change internal thoughts, you must practice visualizations, affirmations, and imagery. When someone looks for externalization, you must say positive words out loud. When someone says something out loud, it is ten times more powerful than if they think it. Negativity is a multiple of four to seven times than positivity. So, if you say something out loud, it is 10x, but if you say something negative, it is forty to seventy times more likely that it will happen or cause a negative result than if you just didn't say anything.

Positive thinking doesn't mean avoiding or denying your feelings when they are negative. If you're going through a hard time, embrace it, find a solution and move on.

The following exercises will help you switch your thoughts into positive ones.

Use positive words when you speak. If you constantly repeat, "I can't," you might convince yourself it's true. Replace negative words with positive words, and negative sentences with positive sentences.

Repetition. Repeat to yourself that you will do everything possible to have happy relationships, that you will do everything possible to have a brilliant career, and that you will strive to keep being healthy. Say it as it's already happening, for example: I am in a happy relationship. I got this. I love what I do…and so on.

Eliminate all feelings that are not positive. Don't let negative thoughts and feelings get the better of you when you are in a bad mood. Even if it is only for a few hours a day. Remove negativity and focus on the positive things in your life. When a negative thought comes to your mind, be sure to answer these questions: Is it helpful for me? Is it making me feel good? Is it helping me to make money? Will this lead me to where I want to be? If the answer is no, change your thoughts.

Use words that evoke strength and success. Fill your thoughts with words of your choice that make you feel strong, happy and confident. Make an effort to focus on these words rather than on those that represent failure and incompetence.

Use only positive statements. One of the most common exercises for positive thinking is saying positive affirmations. What does it mean? Begin to repeat, "I deserve to be happy," or, "I deserve to be loved." Believing in the truthfulness of these affirmations and repeating them continually will impose a more positive vision of your life.

Redirect your thoughts. This method is used by psychotherapists to help control thoughts when they begin to become overwhelmed by negative emotions, such as when fighting anxiety. How can you do it? When you begin to experience this kind of emotion, create contrasting positive images, something that makes you feel better and allows you to keep your negative thoughts in check.

Analyze what went wrong. Thinking positive does not mean denying that something may not go the way you want. Take time instead to understand what has not worked and what has brought you to the current situation in order to avoid future mistakes. Learn from your mistakes and go on without complaining or feeling sorry for yourself.

Forgive yourself. Crying over things that didn't work out won't change anything. Try to forgive yourself and allow yourself to turn the page and move on.

Think of failures as opportunities. Sometimes, the most negative event of our life provides opportunities that otherwise would have gone unnoticed. For example, losing your job could be a good opportunity to start your own business, get back to studying or spend more time with your family. Successful people see failures as an opportunity to grow.

Work on your imagination. Visualize the result of what you want to achieve or the person you want to become. It is a great motivation for you to imagine how wonderful life can end up being.

CHAPTER 3

Dream Big

"So many of our dreams at first seem impossible, then they seem improbable, and then, when we summon the will, they soon become inevitable."

—**Christoper Reeve**

Some people have heard or used the phrase "dream big" without giving much thought to what it entails. In fact, some see the phrase "dream big" as being ambiguous and even a cliché. The term "dream big" is a common phrase in the creative world today. It is often used to inspire and motivate people to be ambitious and to work to attain success. It is what you aspire to be in the future.

Dreaming big is a mental reflection about what you desire to accomplish in life. It means seeking purpose for your life and setting high values and standards for your future self with the expectation of surpassing them. Dreaming big is the beginning of anything you desire in life; it is an attribute of aspiring, self-driven, confident, successful, visionary people, and also, a key ingredient for a happy life. Dreaming big is an important requirement for setting goals. It means reaching outside the normal, visualizing and aiming for a certain higher level than what you are conventionally used to. Dreaming big is the first mental activity that is nursed and nurtured before it gains a physical expression. When you allow yourself to dream big and have bigger goals in life, you also trust your capabilities and allow yourself to succeed or fail at it or at least give it a try to show your passion for that dream.

There is a famous quote from Ellen Johnson Sirleaf that says, "If your dreams don't scare you, they are not big enough." Dreaming big has never been a bad idea, and you do not need anybody's validation before you dream big. You will be doing yourself a huge disservice if you limit your dream because of fear, intimidation or feelings of low self-worth, because you will never know how far your dreams can take you until your dreams become a reality. Take a look at the entire items you use daily that make life easy for you and you will find yourself staring at products that were once dreams to other people. The soap and bath items were produced by a company that was born out of a dream; the same goes for clothing, cars, cell phones, the internet, restaurants, the school system, the train or bus service, the electricity, the gas, the heating system, the airplane, the wristwatch, the computers, the stereo system, the television, the refrigerator. These items where once in the imagination of all these people.

Every successful man was once a dreamer, and every accomplishment was once a dream. The size of your dream does not determine the certainty of accomplishing your dream because no dream is more important than another. When you dream or aspire to be successful, you are sowing tiny seeds that will spring up and become big achievements in the future. If you want to impact the world in your own capacity, it is ideal to start with a dream and gradually work to see it accomplished.

The popular dream of Martin Luther King Jr. of a black man becoming the president of the United States of America is an ideal example of why we should all dream. When he had that dream, it seemed impossible and even crazy, but because his dream was valid, it finally became a reality even though he was not alive to witness it manifest.

Some people are natural dreamers. They love to make things happen and champion a cause while some people have to take baby steps and learn how to go about accomplishing their dreams. These categories do not matter; what matters is that you are working to accomplish your dreams. Your dream may require a combination of physical and mental activities to accomplish, and you may feel incompetent or unable to sacrifice everything to achieve it. You may even feel discouraged with the uphill task ahead but giving up should not be an option for you. You can start small; you can break the task down to little goals and tick them off as you accomplish them. It is perfectly okay to fall sometimes, so go ahead and take a break for a short while but get back up soon and continue your journey.

Unlike people without dreams, dreaming big allows you to stay focused, disciplined and committed to a cause that can greatly influence your success in life. You have to dream to be successful before you can become successful; the mere desire to become successful is a dream or vision about a future reality, one of abundance and a better life. Staying focused on that dream until it becomes a reality will make you successful. Every dream you accomplish leads you to bigger dreams, and bigger dreams means bigger successes. Your success in life hinges on your accomplished dreams. Most people give up on their dreams when faced with difficulty and failure, but if you can pull through the stormy waters, your dreams will give you a platform for growth and success.

Get rid of the judgment of those who consider it all impossible. Shake off the fear of appearing deluded and the fear of failure. Failing is not a problem. It means that you have tried and having tried it means living without regrets. I assure you, the last thing you will want to have on the verge of death, when you will not have more time available, is an endless series of regrets. For example, children always have inspirations and big goals. They want to be astronauts, singers, big entrepreneurs, musicians, etc. They think that they can touch the sky; however, through years and repetitions of being exposed to people who don't think it's possible, they adopt their program, ideologies and beliefs. Instead, they settle for an average life and end up being unhappy. You can't know where certain thoughts and emotions will take you. Maybe tomorrow, you will look back and realize that your great personal revolution towards the happiness you managed to accomplish started with dreaming.

A cardinal element of a person is imagination. Einstein used to say that imagination is more important than knowledge. Researchers think that imagination is not an easy task for the brain. Imaging a scenario involves 12 different regions of the brain. Creativity includes all these regions to share the information and create an objective image for that imagination. These regions work in coordination to create that image. While using your imagination, a whole lot of neurons are being fired to help in the thought process. The parts of the brain associated with imagination are the same that are involved in understanding the social surroundings and then creating pictures of that world through your imagination. Some factors can have an effect on our imagination: the environment, the past and the basic rules that give a particular path to our imagination about how the world works and what and how we see through our lens. Past experiences and knowledge of us or others, good or bad, helps us to shape our present and future and helps us to find solutions to issues we face in our routine life. This is how the creativity in us gets the spark and comes up with new recipes, business ideas, designs, and inventing new games to play. Besides coming up with new and creative ideas and solving the routine issues, there are numerous other advantages to having an active brain with good imagination power. Imagination can also help us visualize and shape our future, like achieving our goals and what we want to do in our life. Imagining things is the ability of humans that impregnates our entire existence. It has a significant impact on our lives and everything we do in it. From the realms of academia to medicine, engineering, and arts, the elaboration of theories and inventions in all professions happens through the imagination of a person. Regardless of the business, imagination influences everything a person does in his life, and there is nothing to feel ashamed about it. The more a person uses his imagination, the better his imagination gets every time he imagines. Imagination is important for everyone, especially for leaders as they have to lead their followers. This allows them to use their imagination to foresee the challenges that await humanity where yesterday's knowledge alone will not suffice.

CHAPTER 4

Visualize It

"If you can see it in your mind, you will hold it in your hand."

— **Bob Proctor**

In our path to personal development, we learn many different techniques and ways to change bad habits and to turn them into positive ones. We learn how to take small steps to achieve our goals. No method takes us to where we need to go. It is a series of actions. One of the most powerful tools you will ever need is the visualization method.

When you enhance the brain's ability to function, you also build new skills. When you build new skills, you are on the road to success, which takes you to the journey you longed to enjoy. Take time now to explore brain enhancement solutions to see what these programs can do for you.

To improve your personal continued existence, you have to consider concentrating on the bigger picture. We all must scrutinize all aspects of our mental and physical states to improve our lives. When we daydream, we picture ourselves in the best or the worse scenarios. This is called "visualization". Through visualization, we can study the issues to find an easier way to move further into the future.

There is a concept in neuroscience called "mental rehearsal." When you close your eyes and you plan an action mentally about what you're about to do, the brain captures that moment as if it's happening in the present moment because our brain doesn't know what's real and what is not. Over time, it begins to install the neurological hardware in your brain, the platform of what you want to become.

The power of visualization is not a new experiment. It is not something that is untried. For centuries, sages have been studying and utilizing the power of visualization to get what they want. It is a proven fact that whatever we visualize, we will most certainly get.

Visualization, or mental imagery, is something we all practice. It is also a very effective tool used in modern psychology. Our physical body is directly connected to our mind, and our mental imagery affects the way we see and operate. Have you ever thought about how powerful your memory is? You can visualize an object, a person, or an event just using your memory. When you dream of something or someone, you visualize it. When you think of an event in the past or something you wish for the future, you visualize it. People can visualize happiness, fear, stress, and desires. Our language is programmed around it with verbs like *imagine, picture, think*, etc.

In short, visualization is the use of your imagination. It is the act of creating visions. It has become very popular in recent years due to the number of publications focusing on this topic. However, it is a method that is highly misunderstood and not practiced correctly.

Do you remember a time in your life when you wanted something so much and you could not stop imagining and picturing it? In the state of daydreaming, you are detached from what is happening around you, focused entirely on your visualization. It is like a meditative state. You are in the moment, in the present. This is when you activate the secret powers of your brain. If used correctly, this power could be your key to achieving your goals, no matter how small or big they are.

One big mistake about visualization is when a person focuses solely on the material goals without having a positive intention. Visualization is not about how much money you want, or how big of a house you want to own; it is more about what you need to do and which habits you need to form to get there by improving yourself and your personal life. Everything around us, including our bodies, is made of energy and frequencies. If we let the negative vibrations guide our lives, we will not see the gifts of the Universe that are being presented to us. Instead, we will keep attracting negative energy and give way to more unwanted life events occurring over and over until we learn our lesson and understand the message.

Some people are magnets for negativity because they let the lowest vibrations dominate them. Some people can turn even the most negative situations into positive outcomes because of their positive attitudes and their ability to persevere under all circumstances. The golden rule is this: If there is no action, there is no achievement. This is one of the biggest misconceptions about visualization. Millions of people seem to think they can turn their visions into reality if they imagine hard enough. This is partly true. If you don't develop a road map and create a plan of action, nothing will turn into reality. You can attract powerful opportunities, but everyone needs direction, and visualization is something that offers that.

WHAT ARE YOUR INTENTIONS?

Is it possible to expect a positive outcome if your start point is not sincere, or if it is negative? In this vast Universe, we are all connected, and each of our actions affect others constantly. This being said, if you intend to harm someone, or want someone to experience something negative, you should know that the energy is like a boomerang and it finds its way back to you, bringing you what you put out. This is what we call karma. Before you start visualizing, let go of anger, fear, and selfishness. If you need to forgive someone, waste no time in extending forgiveness. Start with a white, clean canvas. Let go of all your negative emotions, and let the Universe take care of it all for you. It might not happen on your terms, but this should not be your concern. Free yourself from the harmful energies. Focus on constructive and positive thoughts, focus only on your goals and how to achieve them in the best way possible.

BEFORE YOU START VISUALIZATION

Having a clear mindset is extremely important in this process. Not everything during this process happens inside our brain. To visualize, we need to put our goals into words that are visible and clear. Write down your goals and wishes; make them as clear as possible. The writing process helps us see the big picture and enables us to create a plan to get to where we need to go. It serves as a road map with the final destination ahead of us. Without a road map, you won't know where to go or how to get there. Writing gives you a map of milestones. It facilitates creating a structure and setting goals. It shows you exactly what to do to get to where you want to be. Whenever you feel like giving up, or feel unmotivated, you can always go back and re-read your notes and get back on track.

Imagine living in a disorganized environment. Even the slightest thought of cleaning and organizing seems overwhelming in such a situation. But once you organize your space, you feel empowered, more positive, and motivated and generally in good spirits. Writing gives you this power. You know exactly what your goals are. Write them down and develop a routine to visualize them to see a clearer path in front of you to start acting. Unfortunately, few people know how to properly visualize. With the right technique, you can begin to see outstanding results in successfully attracting what you want, granted you full apply what you learn.

5 METHODS OF VISUALIZATION
COLLECT DATA

In the beginning, it might be hard to visualize something you have never experienced before. Chances are, it is not as difficult as you think. Let's say you want to move to a foreign country and start a new life there. You probably chose that particular country because it means something to you. You probably already read some books or blogs online. Use the experience of others to guide you and help you visualize your dream. Watch You Tube videos, subscribe to channels of people who went through the whole ordeal of going to another country, and get familiar with the steps they had to follow. Then prepare your plan of action.

DRAWING TECHNIQUE

If you are good at drawing, you can always create a sketch or a painting. For example, if you want to lose weight, draw yourself as a fit-looking person. You can draw yourself wearing a swimsuit, exercising, and building muscles. Drawing creates a meditational state of mind, and this is the most important process about it. When you start drawing, you get into that moment and you start experiencing it.

CREATE A MOVIE

One very effective way to visualize things is to create a movie in your head. Write the scenario and control the scenes. You are the director. Try to imagine everything as close to reality as possible. It might not be easy to do if you are in a chaotic or busy environment. Make sure you are in a quiet and peaceful place. If your household doesn't permit you to do this exercise, you can try this when everyone is asleep, late at night, or early in the morning before they wake up. The more you practice it, the easier and quicker it will get for you to get into the mindset and be in your movie. Each time, the images will become sharper.

VISION BOARD

If you find it difficult to visualize, get a scrapbook and paste pictures of what you want to achieve in a year. Make a collage of what you desire. This will help you to visualize better. This is known as a vision board or a dream board; these are very popular nowadays in companies. You can also put pictures over your place or your room that you can see every day and any time. If you want to go to Paris for example, set a picture on the screen of your phone of the Eiffel Tower or somewhere you can see it most of the time. You can use pictures with quotes that remind you your goals as well.

MEDITATION

Mindfulness meditation helps you focus on the present moment and become aware of your surroundings and yourself. It provides mental cleansing and improves your focus. This step might especially be helpful if you are having a hard time visualizing your goals. you can meditate late at night, early in the morning, or any time during the day that is convenient for you.

To make visualizations work, be very specific about what you want. If you want a house, close your eyes, and imagine what color it is, how does it look on the inside, how does it smell, how do you feel walking by the rooms. Does it have a huge backyard? Does it have a pool? Don't hesitate to make your imagination fly. To make it real and more powerful, buy something for the house, something small, maybe a mirror, or decor for the door or your living room.

WHAT ARE THE BENEFITS OF VISUALIZATION?

- Visualization helps you get a clear picture of your goals
- It increases your frequency and makes you a more positive person
- It enables you to be more focused and organized
- It increases your motivation
- It increases your self-esteem and self-love
- It reduces stress and anxiety
- It helps to fight depression
- It makes you a more determined person
- It helps you to set your boundaries and priorities
- It gives you the inspiration to create and try new things
- It makes you more open-minded and tolerant
- It helps you to overcome your fears

- It improves your physical health

It may sound strange, but it is a fact that our subconscious mind cannot tell the difference between a real memory and an imaginary one. This means we can reprogram our brain to redesign the life we always wanted and the goals we want to achieve. The thoughts, emotions, words, and beliefs we load into our brain create our reality. They, in turn, affect our mental and physical well-being. If you can effectively practice visualization techniques, your brain will get in the mood you want it to be.

Everything starts with an idea. The greatest inventions were all once ideas until someone had enough courage and self-belief to work on them and create them. Therefore, ideas and imagination are important. Everything begins with a thought.

When you have a clearer mindset, you will see that finding solutions to existing or unexpected problems will become easier and less stressful. When your brain starts operating on a higher frequency, you will see the world through different eyes.

Daydream and visualize just as long as it makes you feel good. The art of reflection and expression is not entirely dependent upon intelligence and diligent planning. So, the ability to visualize has nothing to do with how passionate you are and how you envision your goal. The art of reflection and expression helps us to achieve our goals efficiently. Human emotions are important passages of energy. Our thoughts and emotions produce energy that is transmitted just like a radio frequency; it is invisible, but it affects our lives and experiences. When a person imagines, he feels inspired and excited, which indicates that he is energetically aligned; this alignment helps and motivates a person to achieving what they want.

Without picturing yourself achieving your goals in the future, you cannot create an action plan. Research shows that when a person imagines himself achieving his goals, it helps him to follow the steps to reach them.

The neurons in our brains never stop creating new connections. It is important to pay attention to what we feed them. Visualization is a powerful technique that has been used for decades by athletes, artists, politicians, and many successful businesspeople. When you ask them, they will tell you that they visualized everything before it happened. You can listen to interviews of successful people talking about how visualization helped them to get to where they are now. In fact, there is a famous song by Travie McCoy featuring Bruno Mars called "Billionaire." This song is a great example of what visualization is about. Actually, this is one of the songs Bruno Mars became famous with. We call these people "visionaries".

CHAPTER 5

Attract It

"Most people are thinking about what they don't want, and they're wondering why it shows up over and over again."

— **John Assaraf**

Nowadays, many people think that the law of attraction is a spiritual thing that has nothing to do with them, since they don't label themselves as spiritual. The law of attraction is neither mystical nor esoteric. The truth is, the law of attraction is pure science: To be more specific, quantum physics, also known as quantum mechanics. It is a theory that describes nature at the smallest scales of atoms and subatomic particles. Quantum physics teach us how to create our material world. Everything that exists is made up of the same substance: energy. Your computer, your car, your cellphone, your house, your clothes, and your body are made up of the same matter. The difference is that every object is made with different elements and works with different speeds of vibration and frequencies. Everything in this Universe is vibrating energy. The vibrating energy of material objects is called electromagnetic energy, making every object act as a magnet, attracting other things magnetically. Our subconscious thoughts are electromagnetic energy, and this is the reason why we can attract every single thing with our mind. The quantum field can create anything, your expectations command to the quantum field to create your material world. For this reason, when you are thinking about something, it shows up constantly, or when you're thinking about someone, that person calls or texts you immediately. You are connected with another object or human being by your electromagnetic thoughts. This concept is known as *synchronicity*; this idea was introduced by the analytical psychologist Carl Jung.

The law of attraction is something real, something that exists. It is verifiable science, like the law of gravity. It is one of the twelve universal laws of the Universe. All of us are part of it, and we have experienced it without exception. We have heard of the law of attraction by our ancestors. Scientists, physicians, psychologists, philosophers, sociologists, politicians, artists, and writers all practice it and represent it in all their artworks. The law of attraction is also in all religions.

As we know, religions are based on astronomy, the study of celestial objects. Babylonians, Greeks, Indians, Chinese, Mayans, Egyptians and many more studied the stars for hundreds of years, which is how they created religions and beliefs. The gods of these religions have different names but similar, or the same, characteristics and powers. All of them knew that there was something or someone more powerful out there. While studying the stars, they found different, unexpected, weird, and unexplained events in their lives, and they expressed them in their books and artworks:

Quran: Allah and the Universe: Universe means "turned into one" or "see one." *"He is Allah, [who is] One"* – *Quran [112:1].* According to the law of attraction, we are going to ask only to the Universe, according to Quran you are going to ask only to Allah, who is God.

There is another book that talks about the law of attraction through the entire book. We are talking about the best-selling book of all time, *the Bible.* *"And all things, whatsoever you shall ask in prayer, believe, you shall receive it."* – *Matthew 21:22.* One of the principles of the law of attraction, in fact, is that you need to ask first, believe, and get ready to receive. And I can keep going on giving examples of every religion that talks about it. The whole Bible talks about it, but it has a different representation.

The law of attraction is the ability to attract whatever we set our minds on into our lives. Whether it is black or white, tall or short, rich or poor, we are all under the laws that guide the Universe. It is this law that turns the content of our heart into reality and materializes it. In simple words, everything we think about comes into being. If your thoughts center on sad, terrible, and gloomy thoughts, that's what you will get the most. Positive and good thoughts will put you under a cloud that rains achievements.

The law of attraction is one of the keys to training your mind to be successful. The law of attraction is one of the numerous unexplainable things in life. Most people do not know how deeply the law of attraction influences their daily lives, and how they can use it to their benefit. We are basically human magnets putting our thoughts and emotions out, while attracting more of what we sent back out. Sadly, most human beings still have a lot of potential buried under the hectic nature of their day-to-day lives. It always seems that it is easier to leave our feelings unchecked, but it sends the wrong thoughts out and attracts emotions and events that are not wanted into your life. Figuring out that the law of attraction works in the sphere of your life should be a cause for rejoicing. Once you figure out the workings of this interesting law, it will no longer be a stranger to you.

As long as you learn and understand how this powerful phenomena works, and you put it in the workings of your daily life, your future will be like a building in the hands of a skilled architect: you. Before you journey down this lane, I want you to stay calm, knowing that it can be applied to your life and be effective. Putting this law into practice has been setting the lives of great people on fire throughout history. The law of attraction has manifested itself to be one of the greatest powers and thinkers on Earth, alluding to it. One of the smartest men of all the time, the inventor and scientist Nikola Tesla, was a very superstitious person, like me and many of you. He used the law of attraction to manifest all his inventions, as did Plato, Beethoven, Einstein, and Edison. The law of attraction is used by current celebrities and athletes including Madonna, Oprah Winfrey, Denzel Washington, Will Smith, Big Sean, Conor McGregor, Beyoncé, Ariana Grande, Drake, Lady Gaga and Jim Carey. The list has no end.

The hardest part of coming to terms with the law of attraction and everything it brings to the table is understanding, accepting, and acknowledging that each and every life decision, either good or bad, was molded by you and you alone. Once you become one with this fact, and you understand the grand key behind it, hope and courage takes the place of the previous doubt and uncertainty. It might be overwhelming, but it eventually becomes great to know that you are free from the cycle of fear that has planted your feet to the same spot for so long. You are exactly where you are because of you.

Once we get these unlimited possibilities that life has put at our feet, we can come to understand that under this law, each individual is an artist. We paint pictures of the life we hope to live, and then make moves to achieve them. If you don't like the particular picture, change it. That is the only mindset a person aiming for a success should have. I see life as a black canvas of possibilities to be unlocked; every stroke of paint to come in contact with it is up to you. You are in control of what the final product looks like. The law of attraction is that simple. All the laws of nature are flawless, and the law of attraction is not left out.

An important part of the law of attraction is that positivity attracts positivity. Our thoughts, feelings, desires, intentions, and actions are all connected, vibrate together, and must be aligned to manifest anything we want. There are many ways to use the law of attraction and to manifest: by scripting, visualization, affirmations, being positive, being grateful and believing. All of them are described throughout the chapters of this book.

The mind is the most powerful tool you can have. Your mind does not control you. You are the only one who can control your mind. Use it wisely. Remember that everything is energy, and you can attract anything you want.

You can use the following steps to manifest and materialize your desires using this law:

Gratitude. Being grateful will help you to attract more. You're telling the Universe you are really happy now with what you already have, and you're ready to receive more of that.

Act as if. Let's say you want to become the CEO of a company. What would you be doing if you were that person? How would you feel every day? Where would you be going? How would you be dressed? Start having those feelings of greatness. Create your reality before it comes. Start acting and thinking like you are already that person. It doesn't matter if it feels awkward in the beginning.

You are worthy. One of the most important things to attract is to become worthy. See yourself as a someone rich on the inside and the outside. When you are rich and fulfilled, you can influence those who surround you positively. When you see yourself as someone who deserves a better life, the Universe will give you a better life. I remember I watched an interview of the supermodel Naomi Campbell where she said, "I make a lot of money and I'm worth every cent." This now makes a lot of sense to me. This is a great example of how this works.

Get in touch with what you want to attract. If you've been dreaming about getting a brand-new car, go and check the prices, go and take a test drive, and buy something for it.

It doesn't matter if you don't have the money yet. Put that intention out to the Universe.

Be generous: Give what you want the most. Clean out your closet and give away clothes you no longer want or fit in; don't sell them. Help those in need. Give some money away to your relatives and tip every person for their services. Don't be scared of giving. The more you give, the more you receive. Remember to give only what you can.

Relax. Put that intention out. Think about what you want to attract every day, but don't get obsessed with it. Trust the Universe. It will come to you sooner or later. Be in a state of receiving. Be sure you'll get it, be confident about it. This works exactly like when you order something from Amazon. You placed the order, paid for it and you are sure it is coming your way.

"If you want to find the secrets of the Universe, think in terms of energy, frequency and vibration." – Nikola Tesla

CHAPTER 6

The Power of Belief

"You can, you should, and if you're brave enough to start, you will."

— **Stephen King**

Life has different colors. It presents us with various problems from time to time. Sometimes, the obstacles are small, and sometimes they are big. Looking and thinking about the obstacles of such magnitude, we start believing that they are unsurmountable.

We can say that having faith and believing are different concepts. Believing means the acceptance of the facts; you believe in something you see or feel, while having faith goes beyond feeling or seeing. You put your eternal destiny into somebody else's decision, but they are both related. Faith is a noun, and believing is the verb of faith. It's the action of your faith.

In order to demonstrate your faith, you must act to change it into a belief. Faith and belief are like a train moving on a track. Both of them need to work in perfect harmony in order to reach their destination safely. Faith and belief are not something a person can visualize through the naked eye. They are more like a tingling feeling when you stick your finger in an electrical outlet; you might not see the electricity, but you feel it's there. They are two sides of the same coin: convince and confidence. When someone has faith or a belief, it means merely the facts convince them. All of us support faith in one way or another. Either we get convinced by the facts of life, the facts of our background and education, or even the facts about what we know about God. Based on these facts, we tend to exercise our faith and belief as we go on with our lives. Being a strong believer who prospers and is satisfied is all about mindset. The mindset and the belief system influence everything in our lives from what we think and feel to how we act and react to the world around us. In order to accomplish our goals, the mindset needs to match our ambitions; otherwise, it might be holding us back from getting where we want to be.

We can describe a belief as the assurance that something exists or is true, and this is something we adopt from other people since birth; it is the same as faith. Our faith and beliefs come from people around us: our parents, family members and friends. It's what we listen and watch every day, that data goes straight to our subconscious mind.

A very strong belief in our ability gives us strength and a positive attitude helps us to find answers to every problem.

Your expectations are not the same as your desires. Your true expectations are in the subconscious mind, and they are translated into your beliefs. If you desire to be smart but subconsciously you think you are dumb because of something your parents told you during your childhood, you will struggle to change that belief. Your subconscious beliefs kill your conscious desires.

We as humans naturally blame other people for our actions, and we do not take responsibility for them. We let other people decide for us just in case we make the wrong decision. "Oh! you told me to do that." Therefore, we like the idea that there is a person above whom we cannot see, making decisions for us, just to feel less guilty when something bad happens. We are co-creators of our lives along with God/the Universe, and we must take responsibility for all our actions. When people believe in themselves, they make sure that no matter what, they are going to make it happen. It is our responsibility to put mind, heart, spirit, and body working together to make our faith a belief, so that belief becomes an action and that action leads to success.

Our deepest levels of belief can help us reach the highest standards of performance. Performing with a conviction plays a significant role in accomplishing progress in life. How much a person believes drives how they act and what they do to achieve success. If your belief is secure, you work smarter, safer, and with greater resilience. Your beliefs can either empower you or limit you. Empowering beliefs can increase performance while limiting beliefs will pull your performance down. This is notably true under competing for pressure or in answer to challenging circumstances. The strength of belief dwells in its ability to do the following things: Belief shapes vision. Belief builds strength of will. Belief generates resilience. Belief ignites and activates the invisible. It sees what has not yet been achieved. Belief sees the intention, and it considers *the path* required to accomplish the goal.

People who are strong support the clarity of vision. They tend to ignore distractions and doubts. They do not involve themselves with what critics say. Because of this laser-like vision and iron-like belief, they win in their mind first. Belief creates the strength of will, and the power of will makes the dominant alignment of the exceptional dedication, constant perseverance, and harmonious discipline. Belief creates flexibility and doesn't just endure adversity, and it gets more potent because of it. It amplifies the capacity to navigate through challenges, difficulties, and setbacks. Having a powerful belief system is the trigger to empower a person to operate at the highest level.

While most people say that our thoughts become our reality, I want to tell you that is incorrect. Experts estimate that the mind produces between 60,000 and 80,000 thoughts a day, that's an average of 2500 to 3,300 thoughts per hour. What really can make our reality come true is our beliefs and what we think about the most. For example, I am thinking about getting a Ferrari, so I think about it every day, trying to attract it to my life, but unconsciously, my belief is that I will never be able to get one because I come from a poor family. I also don't think I am able to get it, nor do I deserve it. My belief is not aligned with my desire. I am consciously thinking about it all the time, but I am blocking myself at the same time because I am not unconsciously prepared.

It is a known fact that our world within governs the world outside. Just repeated thoughts control reality. We can have power over the whole of reality by understanding the laws of belief and consciousness. We can supervise all reality by using the power of true objective existence. You can decide to believe uniquely about what you are witnessing and cause reality to adjust instantaneously or over time. Beliefs that shape reality are beliefs in subjective reality. They can create or perpetuate change. Believing causes our efforts to manifest in our experiences. At the same time, disbelieving keeps them away from appearing in our reality. The purpose of having an understanding of beliefs and reality is to enable anyone to determine authentic beliefs that serve to empower them and create the truth they desire. Understanding brings us power and aims to help people attain a greater awareness of living and experiencing life. For the human consciousness to evolve to higher levels and to revolutionize the way we understand the mind and reality, the power of belief plays an important role. This is what directs every area of life and destiny. That's why we need to pay more attention to our beliefs and do something in order to change them to attract and get anything we want. The good news is that you don't need to believe 100%; believe 51% to start the process of manifesting and receiving.

I share below some techniques you can try to believe in to change non-serving beliefs:

Make peace with the past: I have noticed that all the people who follow self-esteem courses do not live in the present but always have one foot in the past, with regards to regrets or remorse, or in a future full of many concerns. All this time spent mulling over something you can't change doesn't make sense. I suggest you do something more useful: you cannot change the past, but you can choose memories. It is called selective attention. It's the capacity of the human being to direct his mind towards a memory (emotion) rather than another. Have you ever been left by a boyfriend, or been in a sad moment in your love life? From that moment, you will only see happy couples in love holding hands. Perhaps you like a car, and from that moment, you only see that brand

and color on the street. It is not that those situations have suddenly increased, but your emotions have simply directed your attention to these events, discarding many others.

Technique: take a sheet and write the most beautiful moments of your past, episodes where they complimented you for some of your qualities, for an achieved goal or simply for your uniqueness. When you lose confidence in yourself, go and read them all, see those moments again, and implement your list.

Stop being a perfectionist: Your expectations of perfectionism could make you feel inadequate, resulting in an excess of negative emotions and ultimately blocking your personality and thoughts. Here is the secret: we gain confidence in ourselves only after having faced something that is not familiar to us. If you keep waiting, you will not remove the anxiety. On the contrary, you could run into what is called "analysis paralysis," which inevitably leads to procrastination, frustration, and overthinking.

Making a mistake is positive: To start believing in yourself, you must change your perspective on what happens to you. There is no person in the world who does not make mistakes. The difference is that there are those who make drama about it and those who don't. Successful people see mistakes as an opportunity to learn and grow. It is very important to pay attention and to not repeat old mistakes. Stop complaining about your mistake. Learn from it and do not repeat old patterns. Advice: anticipate yourself in case you don't get the result you were looking for. Have a "playful" attitude. Remember that children do not complain because they cannot immediately walk; they are ready to get up and try again thousands of times. Keep in mind that every change and every new experience is linked to the iron law of the learning curve, which shows that at the beginning, everything is difficult, but if you work hard, at the end it becomes easy. To grow in every field, you must inevitably make mistakes, and it is okay. Enjoy the ride!

Don't care about what others think and say about you: Those who are always worried about what others think had parents with rigid teachings that limited the freedom of the child with derogatory and hyper-critical comments. Those with low self-esteem do not believe in their own ideas, or they attribute too little value to the judgment of others and do not consider the search for the last to be subjective. Who does not believe in himself, usually attributes more the value of the sender rather than his own. Relativize judgments and listen only to those that are truly constructive. Tip: read the biographies of people who made it in history. You will notice that they have always been hampered by the masses.

Innovators are lonely people. Don't turn people's voices into your inner critic. Your mind does not always tell the truth.

Make a move: "I can't but the others can." It's all in your head; stop considering others as always superior. Don't think about it too much. Stop overthinking and just do it. The right time to do something doesn't exist. The right time is when you make the decision to do it.

I am tired: People who do not believe in themselves consider themselves to have fewer resources than others: intelligence, strength, energy. They tend to complain easily and love to bask in apologies. This type of people does not take care of two fundamental skills of good self-esteem: self-discipline and willpower. Successful people also act when they want to, and they go out of their way every day with passion.

CHAPTER 7

Change Your Mindset

"The only path by which another person can upset you is through your own thought."

— **Joseph Murphy**

Changing your mindset is a tactic that everyone who wants to achieve their goals should use. Whether you are self-employed, or employed by small or large companies, the change of mentality is a great starting point to take the road to personal and professional success.

Often, we hear about it, but many still don't know well what the mindset is and how it can be exploited. For this reason, it is necessary to start from the basics to better understand the concept and apply it in different situations of life. In fact, the change of perspective towards reality is good for both, for your professional and personal life. It can be a useful and effective strategy while dealing with obstacles with a different predisposition.

To be able to talk about it and to be able to exploit it, we must first define what the mindset is. With this expression, we want to refer, in general, to all that set of conditionings and beliefs that our mind has assimilated during life. This habitual mental attitude characterizes our ways of reacting and acting in certain circumstances. In a certain sense, we can define the mindset as our habitual behavior in the face of the situations that arise.

As children, we are modified and conditioned to have convictions in every part of our life. We spend the first seven years of life downloading data. During these years, the brain is in theta mode, which implies and might figure out how to react and how to carry on. Theta means imagination and can also means hypnosis. The movie "Matrix" is a documentary, not science fiction. A child under seven, is in a lower vibrational frequency in consciousness. No conscious exertion is placed into this procedure. Our beliefs were introduced in us by our friends, educators, relatives, companions, and other persuasive individuals. Furthermore, we structure our beliefs on experience. These modified beliefs are situated in our subconscious mind and work consequently. The repetition of mental programs made in the subconscious mind, attempt to make a change inside our lives, the framework experiences issues changes any perpetual or enduring outcomes. Ninety-five percent of life originates from the subconscious program.

For example, when someone is convinced that he cannot speak in public, he will probably tend to avoid opportunities during which it is necessary to show his skills in front of others. This determines a general insecurity, which if not addressed, will take root more and more deeply in his mind, inducing him to renounce and surrender for fear of making mistakes.

This is precisely one of the reasons why I find it essential to know yourself. Knowing your limits, your fears, your difficulties and being able to admit them is an important step towards the possibility of overcoming your limits. They are often imaginary limits that we set for ourselves. In reality, it is our fears that speak and make us believe that there are impossible obstacles to overcome. Let's start from the assumption that nothing presents an insurmountable problem. Sometimes, what is needed is having the right weapons to deal with it and a little help to take the field and fight.

We said that the mindset is a mental setting that has taken root in each of us year after year. So, how is it possible to change what seems so deeply rooted in us? The most adequate answer to this question is that after having understood what the mindset is, what we must do is put it into practice. In fact, practice is the best way to concretely fix theoretical concepts and to start realizing good intentions. In short, the theory is necessary for the purposes of knowledge, but if it is not fixed by practice, it takes the risk of remaining itself. I invite you to translate your intentions into real and useful activities.

To build a new and improved mindset, it is also fundamental to have a solid theoretical basis. This means that, as mentioned before, we must first know ourselves and know what goal we want to achieve in order to know what to work and modify to get the result. Knowing what the mindset is and exploiting it are consecutive steps of the same process that will bring you success. To arrive, therefore, to have a mindset that is not only positive but oriented towards your goals, you will have to create, through study and theoretical application, a very solid base that will be useful when you actually have to go through the practice. Knowing yourself, your limitations, and the objective to be reached are fundamental steps to be able, in a second's notice, to practice with conviction and effectiveness. There is no definitive mindset.

After understanding what the mindset is and building solid theoretical bases, it is time to move on to implementation. This step may not be so easy and immediate, and above all, it could also happen that you did not immediately put the correct strategy into practice. This depends on the fact that the times in which it is possible to act already in the right and effective way are rare. Each activity and each situation have different tactics. This means that the transition to practice requires adjustments along the way. There is no definitive mindset for all situations, but for every occasion, you will have to shape your strategies ad hoc. The mindset is not a point of arrival but a process in progress, a continuous evolution of the personal way of approaching things. Real and useful activities are your intentions. Obviously, it will be fundamental, to acquire a new mindset, to change it and to introduce positive concepts into your mind that can be useful both in personal and professional life.

I am pretty sure most would agree with me if I say our brain is one of the most complicated parts of our body. But you may be surprised to find out how much control we have over our brain's functionality and programming.

When I was doing my research, I found a book called *The Power of the Subconscious Mind* by Joseph Murphy. This book helped me to really understand the concept, how it works and how to change it and benefit from it.

The power of our subconscious mind goes way beyond our thinking. If you consider your subconscious mind as a bank, its capacity to store coins is unlimited. This could be understood by the fact that when we reach the age of 21, we have already stored hundreds of memories, more than the Encyclopedia Britannica. Although this might seem like a far-out idea, it is true. Under hypnosis, people can remember their memories from fifty years ago with perfect clarity. This is because our subconscious mind is way healthier, and our unconscious memory is excellent. We just need to learn to access it. Our subconscious mind can store and retrieve data if appropriately trained. It's the job of our subconscious mind to respond according to our behavioral programming. Everything we do or say fits a pattern of consistency based on our programming of the subconscious mind. This is the reason behind motivational speakers' success. They impact people to commit to positive thinking and reprogram their thought programs into a more positive progress-oriented manner. Our subconscious mind can bring about a positive outlook on our life when we start focusing our thoughts on uplifting ideas. The subconscious mind is not objective; it is somewhat subjective. It is not meant to reason independently but to obey whatever orders it receives from our conscious mind. As our conscious mind can be made to learn new things like driving a car or painting a wall, our subconscious mind can also be trained to do something we desire. This is another reason harnessing the power of a positive thought process is vital in making the foundation of our entire subconscious thought process. What our conscious mind commands, our subconscious mind obeys. Think of it as a servant who is unquestioning and willing to work day and night to make sure you behave in a pattern consistent with your hopes, thoughts, and desires. Whatever you want to plant in your subconscious mind, may it be flowers or weeds, it will grow; the choice is up to you.

Our subconscious mind has a homeostatic impulse. It keeps our body temperature at 98.6 degrees F, breathing regularly and with an average heart rate. It works by the autonomic nervous system and maintains a balance among all the chemicals in billions of our cells, so that our entire body functions in complete harmony all the time. Our subconscious mind also uses this functionality in the mental realm by keeping our thought process and acting consistently with what we have done and said in the past.

Our subconscious mind tends to memorize our thought process and make notes of our comfort zone. All our habits on how we behave are stored in our subconscious mind. Whenever we do something new or out of our comfort zone, our subconscious mind causes us to feel physically and emotionally uncomfortable. The sense of discomfort is a psychological sign informing you that your subconscious has been activated and working correctly. We are trained subconsciously to act on specific behavioral patterns. Our subconscious mind has been working to establish those patterns in the background without us knowing. Our tendency to commit to these patterns is one of the main reasons why most habits can be tough to break. However, if you learn to create specific designs, you can harness the power of the subconscious mind and purposefully put new comfort zones to which your subconscious will respond and adapt quickly. You can often feel your subconscious pulling you back each time you try something new. Even having a thought about doing something new from what we have been accustomed to will make us feel uncomfortable and uneasy. This may be tough to do at first, but once this becomes a habit, it becomes easier. In doing so, we can reprogram our subconscious mind to work in our favor. Men and women who have trained their subconscious minds are always pushing and challenging themselves out of their comfort zones. They are aware of how quickly their comfort zone can turn into a rut.

Your nervous system operates at lightning speed; consequently, unless you change the image on the inside first, the outside will reflect the new you. If you truly want to learn how to reset your mind to achieve better results, you must identify these programs and work on them consistently to make those changes. The two minds, conscious and subconscious, learn differently. Your conscious mind is known as the creative one, and can learn from reading a book, watching a video, or reading an article. It is the source of all your wishes and desires and aspirations. On the other hand, the subconscious mind is the habit mind. It is resistant to change, its functions are in a completely different manner than the conscious mind. Its purpose is to make our programs real. If the subconscious recognizes that there is something in the field related to your current existence, it will attract it to you. This is how and why you hear the phrase "like attracts like." It will show your focus to anything related to who and what you are. What this represents is what is available to you and relatively connected to you.

It is known that self-satisfaction is the enemy of creativity and future possibilities. For a person to grow, they have to get out of their comfort zone. They have to be willing to feel uncomfortable and awkward while having newer experiences. You should know that if something is worth doing well, it is worth doing poorly too, until we get the hang of it. For those looking to increase their comfort zone, unlocking the power of these behaviors by training your subconscious mind will put you a step closer to being able to make the great things happen in your life. Learning new techniques to reprogram your subconscious mind will make you believe in yourself, as your confidence will no longer be challenged by the great fear of the unknown. Most importantly, this will train your brain to work with your life goals.

The more in tune you become with your subconscious mind, the closer you will get to success. For example, you might have an idea for writing a book that has been in the back of your mind for years. With the adequate confidence and power of the subconscious mind, you can take the next step and write that book, rather than just clinging to the dream. It is taking immediate action on your ideas, which is a powerful key to success. Freeing ourselves from doubts and beliefs that are self-limiting is the first step in unlocking the real power of the subconscious mind. You might have read somewhere that humans use only a limited portion of their brains. It might be because a large part of the human mind works unconsciously. This is currently being studied. A lot of our daily functions of the human body are controlled by our subconscious mind. A couple of examples would be breathing and stomach movements. To communicate thoughts between your subconscious mind and conscious mind, you should know how to control and use your emotions. Ideas that are linked to emotions can be conveyed to the subconscious mind with more ease, and those which are backed by a solid emotional state stay there. This is true for both positive and negative thoughts and emotions. Sadly, for some, negative emotions are more reliable than positive emotions. Be careful with the music you listen to, the movies you watch, the people you hang out with, and the books you read. What you consume on a daily basis goes straight to your subconscious mind, alters your perception of reality and creates confusion on achieving your goals if that data is not aligned with them. All this information may empower you or disempower you.

To truly utilize the power of the subconscious mind, you should get rid of all the thoughts that are linked to negative emotions. This should be done by trying to avoid negative talks and eliminating any feelings in our minds, which are associated with a negative state of mind. Negative talk and thought patterns can have a harmful impact and often affect our minds significantly when accompanied by negative emotions. Getting rid of these negative patterns or having a plan to counter them is an essential step towards success. If you imagine your subconscious mind as a writer of your thoughts, when you say things like, "My life is awful," "My body is not perfect," the subconscious mind writes it down and makes you believe that all these things are true. Your subconscious mind doesn't know what is true and what is false; there is no difference whether you believe it or not. The brain believes what you tell it the most, and what you tell it about you is what it is going to create. Therefore, you should stop right here and question yourself, can you afford negative self-talk right now? The best practice to reduce negative self-talk is the counter technique. For every negative thought that comes to your mind, counter it with final positive thinking. For instance, if you have a significant presentation coming up and your mind thinks, "I am going to embarrass myself. I'm a mess," you should immediately counter it with, "I will do fantastic, and the audience will give me a standing ovation." This will counter the negative thought, and maybe the outcome will weigh in your favor.

Another way to control your subconscious mind and counter negative thought patterns is by having an imaginary delete button in your brain. Picturing a negative thought getting deleted, torn off or burned helps the subconscious mind in acting along this way. This is an effective way to control the subconscious mind and to harness its power by controlling the information it is allowed to process.

Have a powerful desire. The subconscious mind will do everything to obtain what you desire. It will open all channels available to the conscious mind to receive relevant information on how to do that. When your goal becomes an obsession, only then you can succeed. Therefore, setting your subconscious mind on desires backed by strong emotions will allow you to experience opportunities in life that are going to lead you to success. The best athletes in the world live by this formula and control their subconscious minds because of their desire to become number one. That is the reason they are winners. The will to do whatever it takes comes from hardwiring the subconscious mind in thinking to do so. They are willing to do what it takes to achieve it.

Having clarity of mind is essential if you want to unleash the power of the subconscious mind. You can learn how to focus on your goals and to stop overthinking all the time. One way to achieve clarity is by putting more thoughts into something. The more you put in, the stronger your vision of a goal becomes. This helps the subconscious mind to gain the necessary tools to turn your goals into reality. Reprograming the subconscious mind always starts with deciding what you want to accomplish, at this moment, and in the future. As the famous saying goes, the focus goes on where the energy flows. Our brain needs direction. Focusing your thoughts on real goals instead of side arguments and tasks and wanting something spiritually, physically, and emotionally helps to reprogram our subconscious mind in training to succeed.

After you decide and achieve a clarity of mind, the next step in reprogramming a subconscious mind includes commitment. Letting your subconscious mind drive you and getting rid of any self-doubt or fear helps in achieving this milestone. Many people have a fear of failure, a fear of rejection, and even a fear of success. We all have concerns that become the most significant burdens that keep us from taking action. By doing nothing and not committing, you will remain exactly where you are right now. You might not get any worse, but you will not get better either. It is essential to accept that this fear will remain in the back of your mind all the time and might push you away from commitment. It is the absence of determination and the lack of actions that negate your chances of success. Negativity based on fear can poison everything you hold. We can learn to commit and reprogram our brain to face this fear head-on. You should confront yourself: why are you afraid of failure? Failure is an education. If you do not succeed at something, this does not mean you failed; it means now you know this is not how it is supposed to work. Next time, you will handle the same problem with a more disciplined approach. This is how we can reprogram our subconscious mind too. Reprogramming it will lead to getting rid of any negative thoughts. If you think of this as building muscles, you might see no change in day one and a lot of pain, but with time and commitment, it becomes a habit and shows results.

The most critical part of reprogramming your subconscious mind has some flexibility. If you support a narrow field of vision, you will not be able to see all the possibilities and miss the most important ones that can lead to unforeseen benefits. A person can never be in control, and life never goes according to plan, that is a fact. Hence having a flexible approach towards everything, learning from past mistakes, and using failure as a driving force will help you push in the right direction. Working with this chain of thoughts is essential to complete the reprogramming of the subconscious mind to unleash its true potential. As long as some progress is being made, you are on the right path.

Reprogramming the subconscious mind is variable. For some, this can take as little as a few weeks to see results. For others, it might take more than a year to reprogram it. The reason why it is variable and takes time is that your subconscious mind is like a piece of fertile land. It will grow anything you sow in it, given enough time and nutrients. Some things are easier to grow than others. Similarly, for some people, the effort in changing their thought patterns is more comfortable, and they can quickly adapt to new habits. For others, it is the opposite. Despite having a different time frame, you must believe in your capacity to make it happen, and it will become a reality. With time and practice, you will understand your subconscious mind in a more detailed way and find progress in your efforts.

To change your life drastically, you need to start making impressions on your subconscious mind. Make positive affirmations. Neuro-linguistic programming, or NLP, is a very effective method to kick bad habits and old beliefs and create good ones. In just one month, we can completely reprogram our brain and get rid of our negative or harmful thoughts, increase our self-esteem, and let go of the things that no longer serve us. Positive affirmations have been used for many years by therapists in cognitive behavior therapy.

There are some key points to positive affirmations. Use the present tense, as "I am living the life of my dreams." The present tense helps you experience your goal in the present moment and eventually helps your brain to stay in that positive experience mood for the rest of your day. Do not use passive voice; use active voice. Repeat these words several times a day. It is better to say them in the morning when you get up and right before going to sleep. This is when your mind is in an alpha state. When saying them, make sure you really mean them and focus on the words. This can work for anything. Make sure the affirmations are positive. For example, if you want to quit smoking, don't say, "I don't smoke." Instead say, "My lungs are pure and healthy, and I am cigarette-free." "I am" are two of the most powerful words in any language. Try it for 30 days. Feel free to choose and write your own affirmations. This technique has been used by many successful people. Mohammed Ali used to say, "I am the greatest" when he was 14-15 years old, which was way before he ever had a professional fight.

This is a hack successful people use. Tell your brain you are already that person you want to become, and let it do the work by itself. Your subconscious mind will do the work for you; you just need to work on your affirmations and not worry about the rest. In addition, use visualizations as companions to all the principles mentioned above to get better and faster results.

If you program your subconscious mind property, it will lead and direct you to your goal and bring those things into your consciousness field of perception. Any repeated mental or physical action becomes a habit.

CHAPTER 8

Be good to yourself

"You are a rare gem born once in forever."

— **Sayra S. Montes**

As an individual aspiring to attain the heights of success, you may become besieged by a heap of things that you have to do and they just keep piling up. The books you have to read, the tasks you have to complete, the training you have to attend, the papers you have to publish, the reports you have to write, the books you have to review, and the list just keeps increasing. In a bid to live up to your responsibilities, you may get stressed out, mentally drained, and buried under work and forget to be good to yourself.

Originally, the term self-care referred to the awareness of the physical, mental, emotional, and spiritual needs of our being. It involved choosing to spend time doing those things that give us nourishment and avoid those situations and experiences that take away energy and happiness. This does not imply aspects of selfishness or narcissism; it is simply a matter of validating your needs instead of minimizing or ignoring them.

You have to recognize that the modern vision of working hard and faster does not make you feel good. You must understand that ignoring your health and balancing your needs is not sustainable behavior and will lead to suffering in the long run. This awareness could be the first step towards a radical change from the conventional model that you were forced to accept in the past. "It is not your health that you must adapt to a sick society." Only by changing your perspective will you be able to make "self-care" a priority. Self-care affects all areas of your life, i.e., the physical, mental, emotional, and spiritual aspects. It means giving every area of your life the attention it deserves to find balance and vitality. Ayurveda and traditional Chinese medicine present a creative approach to health and happiness. With self-care, you take the responsibility of looking after yourself before getting sick. You become aware in order to return to a life of balance and vitality, you must strive to give yourself everything you need.

Being good to yourself is crucial to your success and to having a long, happy, and healthy life. There are deliberate actions you can regularly take that will translate to being good to yourself. We need to take care of ourselves. If I got sick, would I be able to work? Would I be able to make money? Would I be able to play with my children? If we are not healthy, we can't do anything. Even worse, doctors and medicine take all our money.

The following actions will help you to relax, recharge, reflect, and reevaluate:

Learn to say no: You do not always have to say yes to everyone and everything. Be realistic and focus on your priorities. Do not let others make you feel pangs of guilt when you say no. Always refer to your to-do-list to be sure you can comfortably take on a new task before saying yes to it. This will help you shave off some unnecessary stress.

Get enough rest: Relaxing and getting enough rest is essential to your general well-being and productivity. You can be good to yourself by giving your body proper rest regularly; this will make you feel refreshed and energized to take on new tasks. Sleep at least seven hours per night.

Give yourself special treats and nurture your body: Treats are like self-rewards. They can be said to be another healthy way of being good to yourself, and you do not always have to break the bank to have them. You can visit the spa for a massage, go to the theater for a show or go to a restaurant. You can also create a day at the spa in your own home. Breathe deeply under the shower jet or take a warm bath with your favorite salts. Choose a sweet and fragrant bubble bath, use the softest bathrobe you have, don't forget to spread the moisturizer and finish with a nice face mask. It will make you feel at peace with the world.

Accept the uncertainty of life: Things will not always go as planned but that is okay. Learn to accept the uncertainty of life and you will be saving yourself unnecessary frustrations and bitterness.

Be patient with yourself and get comfortable being you: Accept the things you cannot change and be comfortable in your skin. Doing the opposite will be emotionally and psychologically straining, and you do not want that for yourself.

Leave your past mistakes behind and avoid dwelling on them: Mistakes happen, and they are a part of life, but dwelling on your past mistakes will be a disservice to yourself and your future. Learn to leave them behind and only pick the lessons they taught you.

Seek help when you need it: You can do so much alone, but you can do so much more when you get help. Seek help from trusted individuals or organizations when need it. It could be medical help, career help, social welfare, or any form of help you need. There are always people willing to help; you do not have to do it all on your own.

Respect yourself and show integrity in all your dealings: This will keep off a lot of drama and embarrassments.

Regularly review your general finance: Take care of your expenditures, savings, investments, and assets and seek professional advice on how to improve your finances.

Nourishment. Your body needs healthy food to have enough energy, even if sometimes you eat too many carbohydrates and fatty foods to try to control stress. Consume nutritious food, always stay hydrated, minimize alcohol and caffeine consumption, and minimize consumption of sugars and refined foods. Avoid toxic and fat-rich foods because they remove energy. Recognize that whatever you eat today, it will become part of you. Commit to giving your body the nourishment it needs to sustain health and balance. Nourishment is also that which consists of everything that comes in contact with you through the 5 senses: sight, hearing, smell and taste. Experiences, emotions, and sensations will become part of you as much as the food you ingest. Manage your awareness and choose only those experiences that bring health and nourishment to your life.

Exercise. Our ancestors certainly did not stay in their homes all day; they led an extremely active life. They hunted, cultivated the land, and moved from one place to another. In the same way, in the present days, our body needs to move, both to keep healthy and balanced to maintain our own biological energy and vitality. You can practice yoga, martial arts or other disciplines based on mindfulness. Go to the gym, do boxing, go for a run, take a walk, ride a bike, or swim. Unleash your physical potential. Give your body the movement it needs; this can help you to have a better and powerful performance, and it also delays aging.

Talk nicely to yourself: Don't listen to the negative things people say, such as "You're fat," "You're so stupid," "You're not worth it." Think about yourself as a gem. Talk to yourself how you talk to someone you love and appreciate, and cheer yourself up. Program your brain with positive self-talk. Stop letting others reprogram your mind. Evoke positive statements about yourself: "I am great, I am wonderful, I am amazing, I am smart, I am creative, I am courageous."

CHAPTER 9

Environment

"The fastest way to change yourself is to hang out with people who are already the way you want to be."

— Reid Hoffman

Successful people pay attention to whom they spend time and hang out with. It is about our interaction with others and the people we allow ourselves to enter our lives. Have you ever thought about how others shape your existence? The influence of those around us is so strong, subtle, and gradual that we often don't even realize how it can affect us. Think about it: from an early age, this power is very influential, and intuitively, every parent knows it. Parents constantly tell their children they don't want them to go with "those kids" because they know (intuitively) that boys (and adults) become the people they hang out with the most. This is why it is so important to spend time with people you want to become like. If you want to be more successful, you need to start hanging out with successful people. Your friends are your future.

Abandon the "negative people club." Avoid people from your past. They already had their opportunity. There is nothing wrong with saying hi to an old friend, but if that person is not your friend anymore, that is for a reason. This applies to exes, co-workers, and family members also. The past cannot be in your present or future. Stop allowing people who talk behind your back to stay in your life. Keep your distance, wish them the best and kiss them goodbye.

To avoid wasting time on "wrong people," start by asking yourself these basic questions: Who do I spend time with? What kind of influence do these people have on me? Is this relationship good for me? Is it positive and constructive? Or is it negative and destructive? Do my current acquaintances help me grow in the direction I have chosen for myself? When you have finished this analysis, try to get away from people who only have a negative influence on you. This is a difficult step to take, especially when the people in question are family members or loved ones. But if they are destructive to your well-being, you must stay away from them.

Are there people in your life who constantly complain and blame others for their circumstances? Are there people who always judge others, spread derogatory gossip and comment on situations negatively? Are there people in your life who, simply by calling you, can bring tension, stress, and disorder to your day? Are there "dream thieves" who tell you that your dreams are impossible as they try to dissuade you from believing in your goals and pursuing them? Do you have friends who are constantly trying to get you down to your standards? If so, then it's time to find new friends and new people to hang out with and learn from. It's better if you spend some time alone rather than spending it with people who hold you back with their victim mentality and their mediocre standards.

Make a conscious effort to surround yourself with positive people who are able to value and uplift, people who believe in you, who encourage you to make your dreams come true and applaud your victories. Surround yourself with people who think in terms of possibilities, winners, and individuals with stimulation. Examine the priorities you've given yourself in life. This will inspire you to spend more time with the "right people."

A practical and effective strategy to surround yourself with successful individuals is to attend places where you can find successful people. It's not that difficult! Join an association or organization (of any nature: cultural, social, political, or religious) whose mission you are passionate about. Volunteer for leadership positions whenever you have the opportunity. Attend lectures, symposia, courses, seminars, counseling centers, camps and retreats held by those who have achieved what you want to achieve. Try to insert yourself and carry out some tasks in the social context of your interest. It's not complicated at all, and once you get into the "right environments," you will get successful people sharing knowledge, experiences and smart strategies to you. If you approve them, put them into practice. Experience what they do by doing. If their new ways of thinking and behaving work, adopt them. If they do not work, abandon them and continue seeking and experiment.

How are successful people great for your life?

They increase our personal ambitions. Spending time with successful people helps to raise personal standards: when you are surrounded by ambitious people with clear goals in mind, it becomes natural to start thinking about your goals too.

They help us to adopt positive habits. There are aspects that can be improved in everyone's lives. Do you have difficulty finishing your homework on time? Well, it's time to surround yourself with people who are able to do it without problems. Do you always feel unprepared for more complex exams? It's time to start studying with the best. The positive influence of people around us leads us to gradually adopt positive behaviors and to put aside bad habits.

They improve our performance. Spending a lot of time with people who are attentive to performance will help strengthen the foundations of ours. Just like positive habits, we will begin noticing the change in our goals that will begin to be more focused on improving performance and making more informed decisions. This could have consequences for our future.

We can ask them for advice. Often, we find ourselves thinking about how much we would like to really excel in something, but we are not sure how to do it.

They help us become more confident with ourselves. Surrounding ourselves with people who positively influence us has an effect on our well-being. Success-oriented individuals know better than anyone else how much success depends on maintaining positive situations. They often talk about useful concepts and ways to improve things. This environment can only have a constructive effect on us, especially in encouraging us to think positively. These are the people who increase our confidence in ourselves.

Remember that hanging out with the right people will take you to the place you want to be. Don't forget to avoid people from your past and people who have something negative to say about you. Never listen to people who haven't achieved what you want to and to people who cannot dream big.

CHAPTER 10

Goal Setting

"Make each day count by setting specific goals to succeed, then putting forth every effort to exceed your own expectations."

— **Les Brown**

Goal setting is a generally accepted concept in the world today. Goals are set in almost all aspects of life: New Year's goals, health goals, financial goals, academic goals, fitness goals, relationship goals, business goals, etc. Goal setting has become a way of life and the way things get done, because it is strongly linked to performance and productivity. Goal setting is at the center of accomplishing success, but despite this, some people still struggle with their goals or fail at achieving them, and this brings us to what exactly goal setting is all about.

Goals do not always have to be complex or abstract; they could be as simple as learning ten new words every week. An ideal goal is one that you feel passionate about and emotionally committed to accomplishing.

There are several effective goal setting guides, principles, and strategies all over the place for anyone to choose from. These guides help individuals or organizations set and monitor their goals until they are achieved. The SMART guide offers a framework in setting goals that is measurable, realistic, and suited to your abilities. SMART is an acronym for specific, measurable, achievable or attainable, relevant and time-specific.

S - Specific: When setting goals, it is of utmost importance to be as specific as possible. This, according to research, is often the difference between goals that are bound to be achieved and goals that may become difficult to achieve because of the open-ended nature of the goal. When setting specific goals, you have to answer some questions about your goal, questions such as, what do I want to achieve? Why do I want to achieve that? Where will I get help if I need help in achieving this goal? When do I hope to achieve this goal, and how will I know that I have achieved this goal? An example of a specific goal is, "I want to save six hundred dollars in three months so that I can pay off my credit card debt. To achieve this, I will draw up a budget and cut out all frivolous and spontaneous spending; I will get a savings plan and stick to it; I will work an extra hour to earn extra pay and I will use coupons for my purchases."

M - Measurable: Tracking your progress makes it a lot easier to stay motivated and committed to achieving your goal. Consider the example of saving six hundred dollars; you can measure your progress by checking your savings account at the end of the first month. If you have at least two hundred dollars remaining after taking out money for other basic expenses, then you are on track and there is hope that your goal will be realized. This means that your goal can be measured.

A - Achievable/Attainable: To avoid disappointment and frustration, you must ask yourself: is this goal really achievable or attainable? Inasmuch as you are encouraged to dream big, it is necessary to ensure that your goals are realistic and achievable. Your goals must be realistic and not impractical. They must be sensible and worth the effort that will be put in to achieving them. Back to the instance of working with the same goal of saving six hundred dollars, if you are jobless without any means of earning some pay or you earn very little pay, it will be unrealistic to set a goal of saving that amount knowing that you may likely not attain it. Thus, your goal should be focused on getting a job or a better job first. There should be a balance between the effort required to achieve a goal and the challenge posed by the goal. The reward gained from the attainment of a goal should be worth the effort that was put into attaining the goal.

R - Relevant: Knowing why you want to set and achieve your goal will help you decide if your goal is relevant or irrelevant. How will this goal impact my life and the people around me? Is this goal something I really want to achieve or am I setting this goal under any pressure to prove myself? These are some questions you should ask and give critical answers to avoid setting irrelevant goals. Working with the example of saving up to pay off debt, you may ask yourself: will paying off my debt bring me fulfillment and peace of mind, and will it help me focus on bettering my life? When you finally reach this goal, if it was relevant, it is going to be something you appreciate and feel proud of achieving.

T - Time-specific: An ideal goal is one that includes a clear and achievable timescale. Setting deadlines will help you stay focused and on track to achieve your goal. For example, the goal of saving six hundred dollars in three months is bound by time; at the end of three months, you should be able to know if you have succeeded with your goal or not. Setting a deadline that is unrealistic and unreachable can lead to frustration and disappointment.

Failure to achieve a set goal may stem from a combination of factors or environmental conditions that may not support the achievement of the goal. These factors include the following:

- Lack of commitment to the goal – you cannot achieve a goal you are not committed to.

- A poorly set goal and an unrealistic goal – a goal not properly set will lead to frustration and abandonment.

- Physical factors – loss of good health or in some extreme cases, death.

- Mental factors – the inability to understand what it takes to achieve a goal.

- Socio-economic factors – lack of necessary resources or drastic changes in government policies can adversely influence a set goal.

- Environmental factors – natural disaster, war, and insecurities can negatively influence the ability to achieve a set goal.

Benefits of goal setting

- Goal setting provides direction and focus; it helps you identify what is necessary to complete the required tasks to avoid a waste of time, effort, and resources.

- Setting goals will give you control over your future as you can determine what you hope to happen.

- Setting goals will give you a clear focus on what is important and will help you channel your energy and resources to achieve your goal.

- When you set a goal and achieve it, it will give you a sense of fulfillment and satisfaction.

- Setting a goal will give you a mental boost and motivate you until you accomplish the goal.

- Everyone loves to win in life; when you set a goal, you will have a sense of purpose in life, and this can positively influence your psychological well-being.

- Goal setting helps you streamline your options and gives clarity in decision making.

Successful people have long discovered the concept of goal setting and have used it for their own benefit. Attaining success is almost impossible without setting goals and working to achieve the set goals. When you set a goal and achieve it, it can count for success. Goal setting acts like a framework within which the activities that lead up to success flow. It is the tool that helps you break down and plan all that it will take you to achieve success and will also serve as a guide to achieving success. It is very important for people to set goals every day. That's how you keep on track. A person without a goal is a person with no direction.

To set goals, write down your goals on a notebook. List them and read them three times. If you don't have enough time, write them down once and read them every day. When you write your goals down, you activate both parts of your brain: the imaginative right hemisphere, and the logic-based left hemisphere. This is well-known in the business community among CEOs and successful people in general who use this technique to stay on track. Successful people in general write down their goals in the morning or before going to bed. Make sure to understand and feel every goal you want to achieve.

CHAPTER 11

Go Hard or Go Home

"If you haven't found it yet, keep looking."

— **Steve Jobs**

Consistency evolves into habits, and it is the key to success. Habits are formed from the daily actions we take, and these actions eventually bring success. What we do once, without revisiting it again, does not shape our lives in any way; it is what we do constantly and consistently that matters. Pursuing success without a means of sustaining your performance will definitely lead to undesired outcomes. Consistency is one of the virtues in this world that is difficult to sustain if not regularly paid attention to. Consistency is building discipline towards whatever area you find yourself to produce a favorable outcome. People who live by this discipline are paid with success and achievement since they radiate persistent focus. A lot of people usually disregard the power of consistency in achieving their goals.

Consistent effort stimulates strong neural networks in the brain. These grooved networks assist in building strong connections in the thinking box's synaptic connections, which in turn, fine-tunes your concentration on a particular work at hand or goal. When you give a goal inconsistent effort, the brain does not get enough stimulation to create strong habits. Consistency gives to your brain therapy and right connections due to repeated and prolonged use. Consistent effort and the right attention make your brain pinpoint the target—which is the success you hope to achieve—and lock it in. Consistency is seen as the ability to keep persistent effort in whatever you are doing despite external distractions. Repetition breeds consistency. Repeated effort will definitely result in the outcome you desire and will become a habit. It usually molds character and sharpens thinking and the mind, leaving the wielder smart and quick. Consistent people usually end up as triumphant human beings, with an unshakable drive to always do more. It is all about discipline. In your journey to being consistent to achieve success, you should have your feet firmly planted on the ground and be able to stand by whatever you want. Never take the lower route, and you'll get the necessary rewards.

Hard work is definitely the grand key to success. It is just one of those virtues that a human being must never cease to posses; you simply can't go without it. Now, we're not talking about mere hard work; we're hammering on the focused, consistent, and persistent hard work. In a nutshell, this means casting distractions side, going the hard and legitimate way to achieve results and success, as well as being patient and trusting the process.

A hardworking person will always change strategies and try something new if need be. It is all about working towards the grand price—everything else be damned. There is no luck or magic when it comes to success; it involves strategic and right actions in the right direction. That is the only way to get there. If success were free and easy, the whole world would possess it. Strategic deep thinking, relentless effort and consistency are what make it such a scarce commodity possessed by only the intelligent. Every successful individual, no matter the circumstances of birth, has put in a significant amount of hard work before reaching that place. It is only fair, because success is the reward you get for hard work. Hard work helps to build discipline and to sustain it.

There is a basic attitude that makes a huge difference in determining the result of our behavior: whether or not we content ourselves with mediocrity. Doing less effort, leaving things halfway if nobody realizes it, aiming for something without worrying about the quality of what we offer, and wanting easy success are all symptoms of a society that is content with mediocrity. But where can we start to change this direction? First of all, by not accepting mediocrity in our lives, in terms of relationships with others, in work, in affections, in tastes and in gestures. Strive to be completely present, aware, and able to calibrate your behavior and your words to always give the best of you.

It is well known that nowadays, this generation seeks for success without working. They want easy stuff. People spend more time trying to look successful without being successful. They look for instant gratification instead of working hard and getting a taste of success at the end of the journey. We teach in schools that being in 5th place is okay. We give prizes to the students just because and not for being great. That's why most of your friends are not that successful. All of them have average jobs and average lives. The truth is that being successful doesn't happen overnight. Having a business requires a lot of daily work. Improving your communication skills requires daily practice. Getting rich won't happen by tomorrow, unless you win the lottery, but that also requires a lot of tries. Learning a new language requires daily practice as well. You want to get some abs? It might take you months or years working on your physique and keeping a healthy diet. Doing small moves every day is what takes us to the peak of the mountain. Consistency is the definition of hard work. Hard work doesn't mean difficult, but it means you have to put that work in progress on a daily basis. You track and measure the progress until you find yourself getting amazing results. Your success may come within months or even years. Just stay on track and enjoy the process of improving and learning. Success will come by taking action consistently and progressing over time. Just look around you; pay attention closely to those who are extremely successful. You can observe their daily progress and realize it is not something glamorous; they do the things most people don't and won't do. They work very hard, they wake up early, they work out, they learn, they read, they work and they do it over and over again. They do whatever it takes to get to where they want to be. Success is progressive realization; you are consistent and make incremental improvements every day. Trust and love the process.

CHAPTER 12

Take a Break

"Research shows that we need to take a break and decompress so we can be at our best at work—and at home. Maybe we should ask if the life we're working so hard to create is fun to live? When's the last time you disconnected and took a vacation?"

— Tina Hallis

For those who are used to constantly being on the move, it is easy to forget what real relaxation is and what are the ways to reach it and to feel really rested. Too much school is bad; too much work is exhausting. Everything is about balance.

If your current lifestyle is too hectic and this makes you tired and stressed, why not try to slow down? Slowing down essentially means finding a personal rhythm that allows you to fully enjoy every single moment of your life, to exist here and now without moving with constant anxiety and frenzy towards the next task or the next goal. Slowing down means taking all the time you need to appreciate what you are doing right now, whatever it is. It means focusing and dedicating yourself completely to the person you are talking to; it means freeing yourself from the obsession with the phone and emails; it means living in simplicity and enjoying the small pleasures that already fill your life, but you don't even notice. Slowing down means focusing on one activity at a time, dedicating attention, and love to it, instead of trying to juggle multiple activities at the same time without focusing on any of them.

Relaxation is the most effective weapon against stress. It is essential to find at least a few minutes every day to devote to true and healthy relaxation, but few of us do it, ignoring the repercussions that this behavior can have on our lives. A succession of hectic days, without a moment's pause, leads to an increase of stress, and being stressed means having less concentration, less energy and more prone to bad moods, without mentioning the damage that excessive stress brings to health. Those who do not have time to experiment and find the relaxation activity that suits them the best can still try to build a small oasis of peace, even during the most challenging days.

We tend to think that sitting on the sofa watching TV is the quintessence of relaxation, but it isn't for everyone, including myself. Some people find it more beneficial to watch a horror movie than to lie on a beach with the sound of the sea in the background. There is no single universally recognized way to relax; the means and tools change according to every person. It is fundamental to find your own in everyday life. Finding time to take a break means finding time to have a better life.

Do less. It is quite difficult to slow down if you keep trying to juggle countless activities. Instead, consciously choose to do less. Focus on what is really important and a priority for you and leave the rest. Try to live in a frugal way and try to seek fullness in the simplicity and joy of small pleasures.

Disconnect. Learn to free yourself from the constant obsession with the phone. From time to time, try to keep it off or leave it at home. If you usually work for several hours at the computer, try to cut out time intervals during which you can dedicate yourself to something else. Being constantly connected means continually leaving a potentially stressful flow of open information. Social media interrupts you, distracts you and leads you in a state of anxiety and frenzy. It's pretty hard to slow down when you're always busy checking incoming messages.

Focus on people. Very often, we find ourselves spending time with relatives and friends, or we meet with colleagues, and despite being physically present, we are not really there with them. We talk to them, but we are distracted by other thoughts. We are there, but our minds think about what we need to do. We listen, but in reality, we are thinking about ourselves and what we want to say. None of us is immune from this behavior, but with a conscious effort, you have the opportunity to turn off the outside world for a moment and dedicate yourself exclusively to the person you are with.

Admire nature. Many of us spend most of our time in the closed environment of a car, a bus or an office. Often our outdoor time is limited to a few steps throughout the day. Try to take time to live part of the day outdoors, try to observe nature closely, take a deep breath when the air is fresh and clean, live and fully enjoy the wonder of water and the environment. Make sure outdoor activities are an integral part of your days. Go for a run to the park or for a hike on weekends.

Breathe. When you realize you're going too fast and feel stressed, try stopping for a moment and breathing in slowly and deeply. Take a breath, relax, feel the air gently entering your lungs. Take 2-3 more breaths, slowly and deeply. Feel how stress slips away from your body. By focusing on each breath, you will be able to bring yourself back into the present moment and live in all its uniqueness.

Don't do a thousand of things at a time. Multitasking is the ability to perform multiple tasks at once, as if it were one of the best features one could possess to be successful.

Science tells us the exact opposite. The human brain is made to think only of one thing at a time, and doing more at the same time slows down its capabilities, increases the risk of making mistakes and jeopardizes the ability to memorize effectively. Perform each of your tasks calmly and carefully. You will be much more functional. Remember, Rome wasn't built in a day.

Read before going to bed: Make it part of your routine to read before bedtime, whether it is a novel, a journal, professional material or a book. Reading before bedtime not only gives you the opportunity to get new knowledge and insight, but it also stimulates your brain to assimilate and retain information without the interruptions of a busy day.

Sleep well: Sleeping for seven hours every day can prove to benefit the body. It will promote physical and mental health and also help you stay alert during the next day. Getting enough sleep will ensure your body and mind is properly rested. You will wake up feeling refreshed and energized to take on the new day.

CHAPTER 13

Be Teachable

"True knowledge exists in knowing that you know nothing."

— **Socrates**

Learning is a tool to avoid falling into the same error twice. Thanks to the notions that we are adding, we become increasingly wiser. Have you noticed the importance of always learning? As a teacher, I am very aware of this.

Learning is a need that all human beings must adapt to the environment. Knowing the environment around us and being able to decide, makes us much more sensible and gives us the opportunity to feel freer than when we ignored that particular detail. There are many ways to encourage learning, and all of them have a common denominator, which is to add knowledge, so little by little, we know how to develop better. Thanks to the small details and the attention we put into our daily lives, we make our enthusiasm bigger and bigger. The phrase "knowing will set you free" could go hand in hand with learning. When you know something, it is because you have learned it before, and if you value what you know at that moment, you will eventually realize the importance of something as valuable as what you will no longer forget so you can also take advantage of it. These are some advantages of having the habit of learning:

Ability to decide. Learning leads us to know. When we know, we formulate different types of hypotheses. Thinking about what suits us. Considering the different options we have is a guarantee that things can work out well for us. Making decisions or considering other alternatives is part of us, and thanks to this, we are, even unconsciously, much happier.

We gain responsibility. Learning makes us responsible. When we know the consequences that any of our actions can have, we fight to eradicate what we did wrong. The goals we set are more personal, and we like to share them with certain people who know how to value our satisfaction and share it with others who also care.

Social skills. When we are learning, normally we do it with other people. Social skills will be fostered in this regard and will make us much more active with respect to any idea we have in mind. Social interaction is something all living beings need; we must enhance learning from here.

How can I learn today? What can I learn today? We must be aware that learning is in all of us. No matter what you want to know or the way you seek to get the information, over time, we realize the possibilities we have just by looking around.

Academic studies are made to teach us a series of guidelines and subjects that will serve us for our professional projection. They delight us with some aspects of life that we must have and oblige us that from here, we get the maximum benefit that exists. People can learn at any time and with all the situations we imagine. From each event, we can get something to start the adventure of knowledge. Sometimes, it doesn't matter what we have taken out (good or bad). The important thing is to be aware that there is something we have taken.

The learning process of the human being is something that must take place throughout life. We are constantly learning, and learning provides us intellectual and cultural growth, and it is essential to grow as people. Reading, researching, studying, taking an interest in a topic, and exploring it... All this makes us learn and helps us face all the different situations that arise in our lives. Curiosity is a characteristic of the human being, and it is quite possible to develop it to achieve our personal growth. We always have things to improve, concerns to solve, skills to acquire and improve, and goals to achieve, and for this, we need to have the will to move and to achieve all our goals. On many occasions on our path to personal growth, we find ourselves with brakes or limitations that can make us give up on our dreams, and with it, we give up everything for what moves us. You have to break your fears; many of them are unfounded, and they are nothing but beliefs that we have about ourselves that are not true. The limitations are only in your mind.

We must remember that it is key to learn something daily as a part of the growth and human being improvement and evolution. The sad part is that many people think they know it all, and they're wrong. There is nothing bad in learning or realizing you don't know something. We learn in school and from our parents that making mistakes is something bad. People need to understand that it is really important to stay humble and open to grow. The most important part of all of this, is that we need to know that knowledge is a powerful tool when used properly. If I'm reading plenty of books, the less I can do is putting that information in practice. You don't know anything if not tested. Your good grades in school won't get you to have your dream job, but practice. Always remember to learn, test everything around you and to stay humble during the process.

Humility is a concept that in Western culture is very undervalued, misunderstood, and misinterpreted. After all, seeing life as a continuous struggle for survival to win over the other and "steal" the success leads to wanting to be stronger and perfect. We confuse those who choose to be humble in life with those who are weak and do not want to get up. If you think about it, even in common language, we use the word humility to define something poor. A humble lunch is an impromptu meal with what is available at the time. A humble home is an essential, small home. The humility that refers to the human soul, however, has nothing to do with poverty and at the same time, it has nothing to do with modesty.

It is precisely here that the turning point takes place: being humble means giving light to one's humanity through the opening and meeting with the other. We can be the person we are today only thanks to the presence of others in our lives. Without them, we wouldn't be anyone; we could never be alone with ourselves enough to be happy.

Learn to practice humility and be teachable. Being humble in life does not mean feeling inferior or having a passive and submissive attitude. It is not equivalent to silently undergoing the force of those who want to trample us, but it means opening the window of the heart to look out on a world to discover, which leaves you amazed and breathless, thanks to its hidden surprises among the simplest things. How many mistakes have you made in your life? Look at the world with the eyes of a child; choose the path of humility to arrive at your frailties and your limits.

The following tips will help you to practice humility and be open to learn:

- Always remember that success is temporary; it should be considered a journey and not a destination, so if you distract yourself or rest on your laurels, all your advantage will be lost.
- Always remember your roots, where you came from and what you learned and achieved along the way.
- Understand your limitations, always remembering that as talented as you are, there is usually someone who can do something better than you.
- Admit your mistakes, because even if nobody likes it, the more you are willing to say "I was wrong," the closer you are to humility.
- Accept the judgment of others, since it is easy to recognize that mistakes are made and that you are not always right, but it is a little more difficult to be able to recognize that in many people who do not agree when you are right.
- Appreciate the talents and qualities of others, looking at others, their diversity and the things they know how to do, so that you understand that, regardless of your likes and dislikes, you may find surprises.

- Praise others, because to compliment them is the surest way to break pride or overcome envy for the talent of others.
- Help others succeed, remembering that pride accumulates knowledge and resources, while humility shares them, pushing others along the ladder of success.
- Learn from others, because, recognizing that they are ahead of you is a very good way to appreciate their value.
- Do not feed your ego basking in your successes, isolating yourself from reality and relating yourself only with people who always say yes to you.

What is your relationship with humility? Have you already let it into your life, or do you keep it at a distance? Are you constantly learning, or do you consider yourself Mr. Know-It-All?

Remember that being successful is not about how many degrees you possess. Many people didn't even finish school and they are great at what they do. Focus on learning skills, practice networking, and learn from the best to become the best. Challenge yourself, read a book per week. Prepare yourself to outstand from others, but never forget your roots and who you are. Keep your feet on the ground.

CHAPTER 14

Abundance and Prosperity

"Money is good for nothing unless you know the value of it by experience."

— **P.T Barnum**

Many people in different cultures have to define abundance and prosperity in different ways. In today's world, we tend to measure abundance and prosperity by money or wealth. The more influential an individual is, the more prosperous their life seems, and hence it correlates to abundance and prosperity. But many intellectuals of our past were free of material things, and they were still considered powerful and happy, like Aristotle and Plato. Although present culture values those who earn the most, nevertheless in history, the most valuable members of society were those who delivered the most. We could say that abundance and prosperity is the feeling of enough and having some to spare.

Abundance and prosperity are not something that can be measured from material wealth; rather it is a state of mind. When we seek to define abundance, the origin of the word itself is essential. The word abundance is originated from the Latin *abunda-re*, meaning "to overflow. The word prosperity is derived from the Latin phrase *prospera-re*, meaning "to render fortunate." Although today we associate all these terms with money and materials, when they originated, they had meanings that addressed the quality of life. Abundance can be defined as to be fully alive, without any sense of desperation. This abundance does not come from struggling to attain it as a goal itself, but as a natural by-product of experiencing a more productive state of psychological prosperity. The feeling of abundance that everyone should achieve tends to be reflected in all aspects of life, including wealth.

Some people may find that a more luxurious experience of abundance requires that they give up their attachment to a certain level of social status or excessive consumption of material wealth. Real abundance and prosperity are much more than just money. Our newspapers, magazines, tabloids, and television programs are filled by the evidence of the psychological and spiritual poverty of the rich and famous, and this hardly needs to be said here: many who own vast amounts of material possessions, and who are, to all outer appearances, extremely wealthy individuals, do not enjoy real prosperity and abundance. People are never content with what they possess, and they spend their lives fearing they might lose it all. Therefore, when we seek to find the meaning of true abundance, it must be something more than having material wealth.

Abundance states that the Universe is for you and is you. If you put yourself in harmony with the way of the Universe, it will take care of you abundantly. To feel this abundance, there is nothing you need to do. You don't need to acquire one more dollar, get a better job, buy a new home or car, or go back to college. All that is needed is that you become informed of the inner process through which you generate an experience of commitment and struggle in your life and abstain from doing it. Feelings of abundance and appreciation are fundamental to the human being; they do not need to be summed up. We have only to become informed of how we are opposing and resisting this natural state.

Abundance asks you to accept accountability for creating your own experience of abundance and prosperity. Of course, no individual works in a vacuum. It would be impossible to dismiss the impact that the values and organization of the larger society have on us as individuals. To ensure the ever-expanding productivity and consumption upon which its health depends, modern culture actively promotes a black consciousness. We buy things we don't need (or won't) because we have been persuaded that we will be somehow requiring them in the future or be inferior without them. We tend to do jobs we don't want because we have become confident that good jobs are scarce and that we can't create our work.

Thus, even while we want more material things, the feeling of abundance keeps escaping us. In addition to the role that the benefits from the broader society, the commonality arises in having a psychology of lack within the person. The modern system of society poses institutional obstacles to his or her creative development and economic independence. Nevertheless, the final responsibility for the individual's life does not lie within the culture into which he or she has been born. This actually depends on the individual.

Awareness of the more comprehensive social dynamics that promote knowledge of lack, as well as the inner ego drives that unite us to them, enable us to break, once and for all, the chains of psychological poverty and deprivation. Abundance discusses the origin of the psychology of deprivation and how these can be overcome. Ultimately, the system is the ego. Liberating ourselves from the dominance and authority of this system should be our fundamental concern.

There are three main duties for us if we want to succeed in our journey to a life of total prosperity and abundance. The first is to understand the inner and outer forces that plan to make us believe in scarcity and thus to feel inferior. Being aware of such factors will help us to defeat their influence over us. The second task is to develop a spirit of abundance in our lives, observing the gift of life with joy and thanksgiving. In this way, we allow the blessings of life to come to us as a part of the overflow of an abundant spirit, and not as things we tend to crave and struggle for form due to a sense of desperation. To come from deprivation can only bring loss, even when we achieve things we needed. On the other hand, when we grow from the spirit of abundance, we tend to attract greater prosperity that extends beyond our thoughts.

As we transcend in the world from the spirit of abundance, we become a liberating and enabling force in the lives of those with whom we socialize. We can help them see by the example that we all live in a rich world and that they can also free themselves from a lack of consciousness. We can all unite as a human race in a spirit of abundance and create new guides of community and social organization, new lifestyles, and new approaches of relating, based on solidarity rather than conflict. As envy, greed, and opposition flow from lack, so kindness, service, and collaboration flow from a spirit of abundance. It is this spirit of abundance that can be our guide as we start the journey to creating total abundance and prosperity in our lives. If you are expecting to receive, give to others. Give away the clothes you don't use anymore; don't sell them. Tip everyone for their service. Give money to your parents or family members and help other people sharing your knowledge and experience.

Aside from seeing abundance as something spiritual, we must admit that money plays an important part in this subject and is something relevant in our lives. We cannot do things without it. Being realistic, it is one of the most important things in life. Money doesn't buy happiness, but it does help us to get rid of many preoccupations.

On the other hand, you may see a lot of happy people who are broke. But why is that? It has to be, again, because of their beliefs. If during your first seven years of life you were living in a poor environment, your mind is programed to keep living in that way, in the "survival" way. And you seem to be okay with that because you have been related to that feeling for many years. For example, in my own experience, my mother taught me and made me believe that wanting to have a lot of money was something bad. Money is a very important tool in our lives to live fulfilled. Money was created to be used, and there is nothing wrong with that. It's been hard for me to think that I deserve a huge amount of money without feeling guilty. My subconscious mind has always thought that desiring and possessing a lot of money is a sin. When I was a child, I used to go to church with my grandmother almost every day. The priest constantly repeated that I was going to hell if I wanted to possess more money. Funny, right? Maybe that's why it is something I haven't chased desperately the last years, all because of my old and lame beliefs. Lately, I've realized that having money is great. Money is not the bad guy. Thanks to it, I have lived many beautiful experiences. It is a positive and useful tool as long as you use it properly and for good causes. But now that I know this, how can I attract abundance to my life?

- Have a good relationship with money and take care of it. Don't spend it on unecessary stuff.
- Give money away. Give it to those in need genuinely.
- Provide a good service of what you're offering.
- Think "thank you money" everytime you receive money or give money away.
- See yourself as the master and see money as the servant.
- Stay in a high vibration. Be happy and content with your current life. If you are broke on the inside, you'll be broke on the outside. The outer world is a reflection of your inner world.

- Believe you deserve money and wealth. You're worth it.//
- Banish fear of success.
- Get rid of old beliefs about money. Money is good and you can help others with it.
- Write seventeen times on a notebook the exact amount you want to posses and imagine what would you be doing and how would you feel at that moment. Do it everyday for better results.
- See yourself as a magnet, you can attract whatever you want.
- The difference between the rich and the poor, is the mindset. They're always thinking about how to make more money.
- Choose to invest your money instead of wasting it.
- Focus on generating passive income.
- Don't stress over money. Money comes and goes.

CHAPTER 15

The Power of Silence

"Work hard in silence, let your success be your noise."

— **Frank Ocean**

As mentioned before, we are living in a generation when people spend more time pretending they are doing something relevant than actually doing it. It is better for some people to feel successful than to be successful. You don't always have to talk about what you are up to. You don't need to post on social media that you are working on something big. You don't need to let others know about your grind and your hustle. You don't need the world's approval. In reality, most of the people don't really care about your goals and projects because 80% of them don't care about theirs either or they are just simply busy with their lives.

Have you ever had a goal that you couldn't reach, and you don't know why? You were talking about it all the time to your family and friends. You were so excited about it, it looked like a great idea and suddenly, things turned out bad, and it just didn't happen for some reason. It could be a big project, a trip, or just a simple plan.

Psychology gives us a solid explanation as to why this happens frequently. Sharing your goals widens your intention-behavior gap, which is the disconnect between knowing what you should do and actually doing it. Psychologists have been studying this phenomenon since the 1920s. In 2005, a group of researchers at NYU studied how the intention-behavior was affected by people telling others their goals. Across four different experiments, they had people first state the goal, and then they gave them 45 minutes to work on it. For each of these experiments, these people were divided into groups. The first group announced their goal to the room before they started working while the second group kept quiet. And this is what happened: the group that said nothing tended to work the entire 45 minutes, and when they were asked about their progress, they were pretty realistic. They said that they still had a lot more work to do before they'd be done. By contrast, those who announced their goals quit after 33 minutes of work, and when they were asked about their progress, they were a lot more confident and tended to say they were pretty close to completion even though they weren't. These latter groups made so much less real progress because telling their goals gave them a fake sense of accomplishment. This occurs because, again, our brain can't identify what is real and what is not. For instance, when you think about and imagine a lemon, a juicy and fresh lemon, your mouth starts watering.

Another example would be when you have a sexual fantasy. Just with your imagination you can produce physical and chemical changes in your body and you can create a body reaction, even though it is not really happening physically but just in your mind. Your body can feel it as real. Therefore, when you have big plans or a project and you share it with other people who are important to you, the most common reaction is these people are going to congratulate you, motivate you and feel very happy for you; at that moment, your brain receives a powerful positive impact and support. At that moment, you're sending to your brain a similar sign to what you will receive when that happens. You are feeling the process like it is real.

This all can be related to visualizations, affirmations, and the law of attraction (feel it like it's already yours). Yes, that is a way to reach the quantum field and materialize your desires. But what's the difference? When you do it for yourself by yourself, when you visualize it and feel it, you get motivation to make it happen. But when you reveal and share it with other people, your mind associates it with the final result, like it is already happening, and your motivation unconsciously decreases.

However, superstitious people think that when they share a plan or a project, it tends to fade away because of other people's bad energy or envy. In fact, there's a saying in

Spanish we use a lot that represents this idea: *"Never shout your happiness. Envy has light sleep."* We know already that everything is energy. Your words are a big source of energy; either they are good or bad. When you share your energy about your plans and projects, you expose yourself to be debated. Remember that the person in front of you is a mirror of yourself. The way to sabotage myself is letting others know what I'm about to do. My insecurities can be reflected on the other person I'm talking to: "What? A new car? A Mercedes? No way, that's too expensive for you. You won't ever get one. The economy is so messed up right now." And that's how the person in front of you is being a mirror of my own unconscious insecurities and fears. Maybe I'm scared of not having enough money to pay for it. It can also apply when the other person has his own insecurities. That's why sometimes it is difficult for people to feel happy about others when they see them reaching their goals. "You are not going to be a big designer; nobody pays attention to them. They don't make any money. You are not even that good." People start to judge you or sabotage you. Human beings get mad when they see people achieving what they think they are not able to do. It is better to remain quiet and focused. Visualize, feel, and materialize your desires instead of sharing them and trying to prove and argue why they are important for you, or why you are going to achieve them.

The first thing you should note, is that you should always keep your *why* within you. Work in silence, and let success talk for itself; it definitely knows how to do it. A lot of people have issues with continuity, and they eventually falter after any sign of failure.

Are people putting twenty hours into their goals? You simply have to put in eighty. Your reward is in achieving your goals, which will eventually travel far and wide to places where your lips would not be able to take the job of telling the story. The main reason people put their blood, sweat and life into the goals they hope to achieve is hunger. Hunger in this context is directed towards that fire that burns repeatedly in our hearts to keep striving and doing the impossible to achieve those goals. The hunger to be more, to do more, to get more, to learn more, and to achieve more never goes away. It stretches you beyond your limits to go to the greatest lengths and to become the very best. We all have this hunger, but in some individuals, it is dormant. This is because it is only human to try to guard from failure. It is natural.

The first thing you should be doing is breaking out of that cocoon that the natural human nature places us in. Once you decide that enough is enough, you have successfully beaten the first stage. You must then decide to make a change. That is the start of breakthrough. Next, develop the habit of working consistently in silence, while stuffing yourself with positive thoughts, which is the simplest demand of the law of attraction. When you work hard in silence, you build a completely different and better version of you; this "you" becomes an unstoppable force.

The world is filled to the brim with a sea of ideas to be taken up by you—on the streets, in a conference, reading a book, and having great conversations. The only way these ideas become anything to produce success for you is by planting your feet firmly to the ground and developing strategic plans to execute them. The only thing driving you should be that endless passion that moves you to achieve success that speaks for itself.

Success is achieved by working seriously and honestly, with full and unshakable concentration. Your mind should be focused solely on the goal at hand, and not the means to brag after the goal is achieved. Silence is time, and time is value, which enables one to perform at their very best to be rewarded with every opportunity as an experience, which results in rewards in the long run. Silence during a successful process brings intense power. Learning to still the mind brings the ability to make what we desire come to being. A lot of people spend time obsessing over the amazing things that come with success, and they end up wasting time to actually work on those goals. Working hard in silence without distractions and unnecessary "ideas" from people "willing" to contribute to the process allows you to truly understand ourselves and channel our inner wisdom and creativity. The reward of this seemingly lonely path is the success that you crave.

When you work hard and alone in silence, your hard work can get the best of you to the extent that you focus on one part and forget about other things.

Here are some tips to working hard in silence, so you eventually come out with success that speaks for itself:

- You should always try to trigger yourself: triggering refers to when you come in contact with something that reminds you about another thing that is related to it. In simple words, it means coming in contact with an object that jolts your memory to another event/object. Things like setting up reminders, e-mails and sticky notes to remind you about a particular task at hand will go a long way in helping.

- A lot of people working hard silently tend to forget the world around them, and they put everything into what they hope to achieve. Let me tell you something, though: the mind needs time to recharge and to be in good shape in order to be able to function properly. Yes, hard work is welcomed more than anything, appreciated and necessary, but a simple day out with loved ones is important to keep the mind relaxed. Plan an event, enjoy the event, and dwell in the accomplishment of seeing that event becoming a success. Doing this will fill you with that momentum you need to focus and work without stress.

- Self-appreciation can never be proclaimed enough. In the whole world, there is nobody who wants you to succeed more than you do, so learn to appreciate yourself and every ounce of blood, sweat, and tears that you put into making that project become a reality. It is even more sensitive with a person working silently. Why? Because you are the only one witnessing everything you are putting in, so when failure and setbacks barge in, ready to tear you down, you have to be completely ready for it.

- You should always be hard on yourself, and push yourself to achieve better things. Remember that you are working silently, and you are the only push and support system you have. Silently filling your head with the thought that you have accomplished a lot by hurdling through the easy things will leave you unprepared for that success story. Your motivation and passions should keep you burning through the hurdles and give you a greater sense of achievement in the long run.

When you finally have reached your goal and want to share it with others, remember to do it from the heart and not from your ego. Firstly, genuinely share it with important people; share it with love and appreciation. And secondly, share it to inspire, motivate and support others who want to reach what you have reached. Sharing is amazing but we need to learn first how to do it.

Let the results speak for you. Let your actions do the talking. You don't tell people you are great; they tell you you are great. You don't tell them you are the best; they tell you you are the best. Start creating that respect from your actions.

CHAPTER 16

Take Action

"I can't relate to lazy people. We don't speak the same language. I don't understand you. I don't want to understand you."

— **Kobe Bryant**

I know people who are extremely talented, intelligent, smart, and creative. I've seen great people who read every day, those who are a dictionary, those who have an amazing intellect and knowledge, but they don't do anything with it. They keep their knowledge to themselves and that's it. People attend seminars, read great books, study for 20 years in a row, but what do they do in the end?

There will never be a moment in life that is ideal for making a drastic change, because it does not depend on time but on the drive that is within us. When you have the courage to make a change in your life, which at the beginning can frighten you or force you out of your comfort zone, you can discover inclinations or abilities that you didn't know you had. Not all dreams can become reality if one craves it and that's all. There are many people in the world who have stopped wanting personal change, who have stopped dreaming, believing, wanting anything, and no longer advancing; people who are preparing to go to jobs they don't like, people who wake up very early every day to follow a routine that makes them feel bad, people who continue to relate to others they don't want, people who hate their profession, but who continue to do it. When you do this, you are literally shortening the years of your life and throwing them to the wind.

Happiness is not a natural and innate condition. It is a condition that presupposes a search, which often requires courage towards that half, which is more satisfying than the present one, and reaching it makes us happy. When we are happy with ourselves and with what we are able to do, we are even more available for others. We relate with others and with the environment around us in a more positive and constructive way. Each social, familial, emotional, and professional relationship can benefit from our positivity. Perhaps, you have come to a point where no one believes anymore that the situation will be different or can be fixed, and this causes a feeling of loneliness that can arise when one is dedicated to promising and not maintaining.

In the cemetery, there are ideas that have never been shown, changes and visions that have never become realities, aspirations and dreams that have never been pursued. It is very simple to fail in life, but it certainly requires a greater effort, an emotionality under eternal tension and a constant stress living in the constant desire for something and not having the courage to carry it out. Unresolved desire wears out worse than any tension and leads to regret and resentment towards ourselves.

Changing our mind takes a great effort, even at the neurophysiological level. Our brain is composed of neurons; habits are consolidated thanks to the connections that the neurons create between them. To break any habit, you first need to create new healthy habits that can go replace old ones. If old habits are broken but they are not replaced very quickly, our brain will go and retrieve them. This whole process is more frightening than our mind to us, because it requires a lot of effort and a lot of work. Our brain is a very perfect machine, but it loves comfort very much.

Let's find out how many of these excuses you are relying on to not take action:

- I have always been like this; there is nothing to do.
- It's my family's fault.
- I'm too old to change.
- I tried but others don't understand it, and I always do the same things.

- I can't do it. It is impossible. I have a complicated life.
- I have never been lucky.
- It takes too long to change.
- I have no time; my family needs me too much.
- You make it seem too easy.
- When I have solved all my problems, I will change.

How many excuses are you in?

To change, you must act. Action is what allows neurons to create new habits to replace previous ones. If there is no action, there is no change. Using a methodology without action leads to failure.

How to take action in 3 steps:

Know your fears: It is necessary to understand that fear is a physiological mechanism common to all animal species that has the aim of safeguarding the species, of avoiding any situation that may in some way represent a threat to its survival. This fear is our friend. It has kept our species alive for millions of years. There is also a fear that is not physiological but that is influenced by false convictions or social conventions. For example, what will people think or say? The first type of fear, the physiological one, is useful.

The second type prevents us from growing, from leaving the comfort zone to try to follow new paths that could open us to new opportunities. If you have a dependent family, or if you are alone but your whole life depends on your salary, you have to pay a mortgage, a rent, you have fixed expenses, you have to eat, etc., so your fear of leaving a permanent job and setting up on your own is justified. The price you would have to pay is very high. It is your own survival, so your choice to set up on your own could be rash and risky. If you find yourself in this situation, I advise you to start with your virtual assistance business or any other online activity, in parallel. In fact, online activities lend themselves to being carried out part-time, even forever. I know several virtual assistants who do it part-time. Over time, you can always turn it into your main business, or maybe you realize that you can't manage both so you leave it, but you won't have lost anything. At most, you will have invested time to better understand what you want to do. Instead, you ask yourself, "What do I have to lose?" You may realize that it is not so much. By cutting some expenses, modifying your lifestyle a bit, you can still cover your main expenses.

Connect with your passion. Fear, like all emotions, tends to blur everything else. Just like when we're angry and we don't want to feel right, when we're afraid, we focus on fear and forget everything else. We forget who we are, what our passion is, what our purpose in life is. If you don't know your passion, try asking yourself what you would do if money wasn't a problem. You will probably answer "travel" (I hear this often), but this is not enough. Traveling is often the answer of those who are too stressed and need to escape, but in all honesty, there are few people whose only thing they do is travel. It is true that they exist, but they are people who have given up many comforts to face life like a long journey, living for the day. But if this is not your idea, then keep looking inside yourself. Maybe you need a trip, or maybe you can combine work and travel, but what are you really passionate about? Web marketing? Yoga? The kitchen? Mathematics? We all have a passion that moves us and motivates us.

Create an action plan. A plan of action is really important to your success. One way to deceive fear, or rather to deceive the mind by distracting it from fear, is to plan. If you take your time planning a new business, your mind will move from fear to enthusiasm, or to motivation and action. Soon you will forget about fear and you won't even remember what you were afraid of! Write or create a mind map starting from your passion and identifying all the steps necessary for the realization of your dream. Whatever method you choose to use, remember that the important thing is to extrapolate from the mind your thoughts, projects, and ideas to create support material that you can always draw on. It is a bit like a cooking recipe: the first time you prepare a new dish, you will need a written recipe, because the mind will hardly memorize all the ingredients, the doses, the procedure. In time, you will have learned the new recipe and you can do it without the help of a text. Your new project is like a recipe: the mind cannot support all the new ideas, which will then increase. One idea will lead to another and the result will be great confusion. Write your recipe for a new life and slowly you will be able to create it.

To get the result we are looking for, we must apply this formula:

Desire + Mind + Heart + Soul + Body = Results

Remember that there is no manifestation with no action.

CHAPTER 17

Write It Up

"Your life is a blank page. You write on it."

— **Donald Miller**

Whenever we think of a diary, we are reminded of adolescence, frustrated loves and a thousand emotions impressed on padlocked notebooks that will be read with nostalgia years later. Without a doubt, a diary is a priceless and very important weapon that not only helps keep memories alive, but also maintains good mental health. Diaries are powerful tools to deepen our lives and pave a better way towards the future.

A diary will help you have a routine; it's a great exercise to sit down every day and write down your thoughts or feelings without worrying about it being a paragraph or many pages, as well as helping your writing and mental organization skills, will put your thoughts in order. It is also a very productive way to spend time. We often prefer to do things that are less profitable, like watching a tv show, but investing some of our free time in thinking about ourselves and what you think is undoubtedly very productive and in the long run will benefit discipline and self-reflection. We talk about self-reflection because the time you spend writing in your diary is a time only for you, during which you can be with yourself and be free to write. This will also give you an excellent perspective to rethink past moments that you can now relive with new eyes.

Perhaps one of the greatest benefits of keeping a journal is for your soul and your peace of mind. It is very important because it gives you the ability to process the events that have been important to you that you may not have considered as such. Processing what happened is very important for healing. Often, we can't trust our memories; having something written will always bring new light to our ideas. It is also one of the most effective ways to clarify your ideas after a very difficult day. There is nothing better than sitting down and writing everything to put messy thoughts in order and, above all, to connect with ourselves and extend our emotions. Writing what we feel can calm us down and help us better understand what is happening and make us feel less confused. Finally, a diary is a good way of documenting the important things in life, recording meaningful lessons that we often forget. A good idea is also to write important questions for which perhaps now you do not have an answer, but in the near or distant future, you will be able to answer and ultimately trace the thread of your story.

Make Things Clear. Writing allows you to reflect on your activities, both occasional and daily. Often it is the small recursive actions that we do not notice that make a real difference in the quality of our life. By writing a personal diary, you have the chance to notice these small actions that you repeat often, perhaps without paying too much attention. Over time, you will be able to re-read what you have written, to clarify your past and better plan your life, having as your starting point your sealed experiences in your personal journal.

See what worked and what didn't. The diary is one of the main tools for hunting for positive and negative feedback. Did that project you started bringing expected results? What went wrong? What didn't work? The personal analysis of your life is much easier with a diary, and it is easier to follow the path you have traveled in recent years to determine what worked best for you. Were your dreams, your hopes and your goals disregarded or were you able to finish everything? What are the activities that produced striking results, and which ones did not lead to anything? A personal diary gives you the opportunity to answer these questions, being a very powerful analysis tool. Writing a personal diary also serves to understand what the elements are, both exogenous and endogenous that are blocking you, so as to overcome them once and for all.

Don't lose your best ideas. Surely, you have had a brilliant intuition only to forget it shortly thereafter. Or maybe you found an idea or a starting point for one of your projects but you didn't put it in writing, because you were sure you wouldn't forget it, but then you did. Finding new ideas is a fairly spontaneous mechanism, but often, what is missing is the solidification of the idea in your mind in addition to a plan to achieve it with precision. Writing ideas, projects and thoughts in a diary solves this problem. In addition to having noted what you thought, fixing it on paper, and re-reading it will give you greater objectivity in judging your idea, and in making new ones emerge. Also, consider that writing in your diary frees space in your mind, space that would otherwise remain anchored to the past. When you have brilliant ideas, these thoughts continue to blend in your head without evolving. In these situations, it is essential to note them. You will immediately free up space to evolve your idea and find new ones.

Say thank you. Including even a single line of gratitude in your personal diary helps you close the day well. However, remember that the recognition of the diary must not replace the real gratitude due to other people who deserve it; it should only supplement the one already dispensed during the day. Always thank the people who helped you solve a problem or gave you a little support. Writing and re-reading gratitude in the diary stimulates you to be grateful for all the things you don't usually pay attention to. How many little things have gone well for you today without you knowingly thinking about it?

Reduce stress and anxiety. A personal diary can absorb your problems and your worries, including anxiety and stress, and it can be used as a therapy tool. Noting, for example, frustrations and anger, and swear words gives you the opportunity to use it as a direct vent channel, which facilitates your personal growth. Personal improvement is also nourished thanks to the knowledge of yourself. A diary allows you to review your past and present yourself if you have been honest in writing.

How to journal

- Write in an orderly manner. You will greatly facilitate your life when you go back and read the diary after a long time.
- Don't worry if you can't write every day. The important thing is to maintain a minimum of constancy without abandoning it.

- Have fun writing and re-reading. Many significant things of today can be amusing anecdotes of tomorrow.

- If you train, write a training diary too.

- Don't write just words; insert scribbles, drawings and everything you feel like throwing down.

- If you are a beginner and you find yourself having difficulty, think about what you would write on social networks.

- Always enter the date; it will be more pleasant to re-read when time has passed.

- Decide which writing fits your personality best. Do not try to imitate a particular style or language. The diary is personal; you will probably only read it yourself, so be yourself when you write.

- Find a good place. A diary can be written at any time and in any place, but if you need a little inspiration, find your place to merge tranquility and peace of mind.

On the other hand, there are different kinds of journaling. Talking about the law of attraction, there is a journaling known as a future journaling or scripting. The difference between future journaling and journaling is that in future journaling, you describe your future life, the life you desire. To put it in practice, take a sheet of paper and write everything in present tense like it is already happening or in past tense. It is very important to start your letter being grateful. For example: Dear _____, I am so grateful and content now that I have my dream job. I am married to the love of my life, we live in this amazing luxurious house, etc. There is no limit for your letter. Try to be as specific as possible. Describe how you are feeling. Describe the colors, shapes, smells, emotions... Write on it daily and see how your life starts changing out of nowhere.

Journaling and scripting are useful for multiple activities and offer safe advantages. They are effective and simple to fill out. If it is not among your habits, try to import it for a month and you will see that you will not abandon it anymore.

About the Author

Sayra S. Montes is a multilingual author, teacher, and translator whose generosity, bold approach, and compassionate nature have earned her a reputation as a dynamic educator. It all started when she was in her high school literature and philosophy class and would spend most of her time writing. Eventually, that initial passion led to the publication of her debut book titled *Train Your Mind to Be Successful*.

Over the span of nearly a decade, Sayra has gained extensive hands-on experience in both teaching and translating. Currently, she holds a bachelor's degree in translation, and she is a certified translator for legal and academic documents. She is fluent in Spanish, English, and French and had the opportunity to study in the United States and abroad in France. She began teaching French in college in 2011 and has been fond of educating others ever since. That led her to obtaining her master's degree in education.

When she is not helping her students, you can find Sayra S. Montes listening to music, doing physical work, or relaxing in the great outdoors. She is also a voracious reader and a lifelong learner.

www.ingramcontent.com/pod-product-compliance
Ingram Content Group UK Ltd.
Pitfield, Milton Keynes, MK11 3LW, UK
UKHW041419180426
11947UKWH00007B/210